CLASSIC DISHES
Made Easy

CLASSIC DISHES
Made Easy

 HEARST BOOKS
New York

English edition published by The Hamlyn Publishing
Group Limited, Astronaut House, Hounslow Road, Feltham,
Middlesex, England

English translation copyright © The Hamlyn Publishing Group 1983

Original edition published under the title
Die Schönsten Rezepte leicht gemacht, copyright
© 1982 by Grafe und Unzer, Germany

First published in The United States by Hearst Books 1983

Library of Congress Card Catalog Number: 83-81055
ISBN: 0-688-02489-0
First U.S. edition
1 2 3 4 5 6 7 8 9 10

Photography by C. P. Fischer
Phototypeset by Tameside Filmsetting Limited in
9½pt Monophoto Times

Printed in Italy

Contents

Useful Facts and Figures

Measuring accurately

Correct measuring of ingredients is essential to ensure consistent results. All measurements given in this book are level unless otherwise stated.

Choosing measuring cups: When purchasing measuring cups you should choose one set for dry ingredients and another for liquids.

For dry ingredients: Buy a set of four graduated measuring cups consisting of a $\frac{1}{4}$-cup, $\frac{1}{3}$-cup, $\frac{1}{2}$-cup and 1-cup measure. Always level off with the edge of a spatula or knife.

For liquid ingredients: Buy a 1-cup measuring cup, the rim of which is above the 1-cup line to avoid spillage. 2-cup and 1-quart size measuring cups are also very useful. Set the cup on a level surface. Lower your head so that the measuring line will be at eye level and fill the cup to the correct mark.

Choosing measuring spoons: A good set of measuring spoons will give you accurate small measurements. It should include $\frac{1}{8}$-teaspoon, $\frac{1}{4}$-teaspoon, $\frac{1}{2}$-teaspoon, 1-teaspoon, $\frac{1}{2}$-tablespoon and 1-tablespoon measurements. 16 tablespoons equal 1 cup.

Equivalent measures

Pinch	As much as can be held between the tip of the finger and the thumb
3 teaspoons	1 tablespoon
2 tablespoons	$\frac{1}{8}$ cup
4 tablespoons	$\frac{1}{4}$ cup
5 tablespoons + 1 teaspoon	$\frac{1}{3}$ cup
8 tablespoons	$\frac{1}{2}$ cup
10 tablespoons + 2 teaspoons	$\frac{2}{3}$ cup
12 tablespoons	$\frac{3}{4}$ cup
16 tablespoons	1 cup
2 cups	1 pint
2 pints	1 quart
1 quart	4 cups
4 quarts	1 gallon
16 oz (dry measure)	1 lb

Can sizes: We have tried to utilize whole cans of ingredients whenever possible.

Flour: Unless specified, either all-purpose or self-rising flour may be used in the recipes. If using self-rising flour, omit baking powder and salt if called for. For fine-textured cakes, you may substitute $1\frac{1}{8}$ cups cake flour for each cup of all-purpose flour. Seasoned flour is flour mixed with salt and freshly ground pepper.

Butter or margarine: One ($\frac{1}{4}$-lb) stick of butter or margarine equals $\frac{1}{2}$ cup or 8 tablespoons. If a recipe calls for melted butter, it doesn't matter if you measure it before or after melting — the result will be the same.

Equivalents

Eggs

5 eggs	about 1 cup
8-10 egg whites	1 cup
12-15 egg yolks	1 cup

Butter or margarine

2 tablespoons	1 oz
$\frac{1}{2}$ cup	$\frac{1}{4}$ lb (1 stick)
2 cups	1 lb

Dairy products

1 cup milk	$\frac{1}{2}$ cup evaporated milk + $\frac{1}{2}$ cup water
1 cup milk	$\frac{1}{4}$ cup powdered whole milk + 1 cup water
1 cup cream	2 cups whipped cream
1 cup cottage cheese	8 oz

Flour

Flour is sifted before measuring

4 cups all-purpose flour	1 lb
1 cup cake flour	1 cup all-purpose flour, minus 2 tablespoons
2 tablespoons flour	1 tablespoon cornstarch for thickening
5 teaspoons flour	2 teaspoons arrowroot for thickening

Sugar

Confectioner's sugar is measured before sifting
Brown sugar is measured firmly packed

2 cups sugar	1 lb
$3\frac{1}{4}$-4 cups confectioner's sugar	1 lb
$2\frac{1}{4}$ cups brown sugar	1 lb

Miscellaneous

1 orange	about 8 tablespoons juice
1 lemon or lime	2-3 tablespoons juice
Grated rind of 1 orange	about 1 tablespoon
Grated rind of 1 lemon	$1\frac{1}{2}$-2 teaspoons
1 lb nuts in the shell	about 2 cups nut meats
$\frac{1}{4}$ lb chopped nuts	1 scant cup
1 lb seedless raisins	about 3 cups
1 square chocolate, unsweetened or semisweet	1 oz
1 square chocolate (unsweetened)	3 tablespoons cocoa + 1 tablespoon butter
1 cup honey	$1\frac{1}{4}$ cups sugar + $\frac{1}{4}$ cup liquid

Introduction

The choice of recipes in this new and original illustrated cookery book is not a chance selection nor does it simply reflect our own personal taste and judgement. We selected the dishes by giving a collection of famous, well-tried and, at the same time, exciting recipes to a number of cooks – beginners, experts, amateurs and professionals – and asking them to choose those which they felt were indispensable for a book such as we envisaged.

We laid great emphasis on the word 'selection', for we were both of the opinion that quality was more important than quantity. The result is a colorful mixture of well-loved international specialties including many different types of recipe – sophisticated dishes, subtle dishes, country dishes and simple dishes – among which we are sure you will find many new favorites.

The book is unusual because the recipes are very detailed. We thought it extremely important to describe the method in such a way that even a beginner has a good chance of success. Each recipe was worked out, tested, cooked and photographed without embellishments, and because the book was written for all those who enjoy experimenting with new recipes but do not perhaps have the courage to attempt Pike Quenelles in Cream and Basil Sauce, Liver Pâté or the supposedly difficult Charlotte Royale, the text and pictures were designed so that the cook can see at a glance whether the result is like that in the photograph.

We tried to describe all the difficult stages in the recipes very clearly both in words and pictures: for instance, making a soufflé, beating a custard over hot water or simply poaching eggs. 'Know how' is just as important in cookery as in any other job and so the simple but necessary steps such as peeling and deseeding tomatoes, preparing peppers and chopping onions are described in exact detail for, if you are not familiar with the techniques, you need far more time for preparation and often fall short of complete success.

The book has been arranged in the classical manner: soups and stews, salads, vegetable dishes and starters, eggs, fish, meat (veal, beef, pork and lamb), poultry and game and desserts.

Ambitious amateur cooks who enjoy presenting their guests with a succession of well-balanced dishes will find many suitable ones in this book. There are also a good many recipes for those who do not wish to spend too much, as well as a wide choice of sumptuous meals, hearty country-style dishes, celebration dinners and simple light suppers.

What is offered here is much more than just a collection of superb photographs of delicious-looking food. The detailed instructions will give you the confidence you need to prepare and serve every single recipe as if you were a master in the art of cookery. You will certainly decide that cooking some of the world's classic dishes was never so easy or so much fun.

We hope that leafing through these pages and cooking the recipes will give you much pleasure and that you and your family and friends will share our enthusiasm for these classic dishes, for it was enthusiasm which prompted us to write this book.

Mechthild Piepenbrock
C. P. Fischer

**Unless otherwise stated, all recipes
are for 4 persons.**

Barcelonessa Soup

Herbs, garlic, lemon and tomatoes give the tasty barcelonessa soup its typically fresh character. It is served with spicily seasoned meatballs and garnished with fresh parsley and chervil.

Serves 8

1 lb piece of lamb
(shoulder, breast or leg)
1½ quarts cold water
1 bunch fresh parsley · 1 small leek
1 stalk celery · 1 onion
2 cloves · 1 bay leaf
1 sprig fresh thyme · salt
freshly ground black pepper
2 cloves garlic
¾ cup lean ground lamb
1 egg · cayenne pepper
3 tablespoons flour
2 ripe tomatoes
3 tablespoons fine soft
bread crumbs
1 tablespoon butter
1 teaspoon tomato paste
4–5 tablespoons olive oil
1 teaspoon lemon juice
1 handful fresh chervil leaves

Preparation time: 2–2¼ hours

Rinse the lamb under cold running water and place in a large saucepan with the cold water. Bring to a boil slowly, skimming off any gray scum as it rises to the surface. Meanwhile, take one sprig of the parsley, rinse it under cold running water and shake dry. Trim the leek and celery. Rinse the leek well to remove grit. Chop both vegetables and the sprig of parsley.

Peel the onion and press the cloves into the surface. Make a slit in one side of the onion with a sharp knife and insert the bay leaf. Rinse two more sprigs of parsley and the thyme and shake dry. Place them in the stock together with the chopped vegetables and onion. Season with salt and pepper. Reduce the heat until the liquid is just simmering and cook gently, partially covered, for 1½ hours.

Just before the stock is ready, prepare the meatballs. Peel and chop one clove of garlic. Rinse and dry half the remaining parsley and chop it finely. Place the ground lamb, garlic, chopped parsley and egg in a bowl and mix together thoroughly, seasoning generously with salt, pepper and a little cayenne pepper. Form into small balls about the size of a walnut.

Roll the meatballs in the flour to coat on all sides. Leave for a few minutes to allow the flour to dry on the surface.

Scald the tomatoes in boiling water for 10 seconds, then peel and remove the core and any pieces of hard stem. Cut in half so that all seed chambers are visible and, taking half a tomato at a time in the palm of your hand, squeeze gently until the seeds fall out. Discard the seeds and chop the tomatoes finely. Peel and crush the second clove of garlic and mix with the bread crumbs. Melt the butter in a skillet and fry the bread crumbs until golden.

Remove the meat from the stock and reserve it for use at another time. Strain the stock and return to the saucepan. Skim as much fat as possible from the surface of the stock and bring to a boil again. Add the tomatoes and tomato paste and stir vigorously. When the stock returns to a boil, stir in the fried bread crumbs which act as a thickening agent. Reduce the heat and simmer, stirring frequently, for 5 minutes.

Meanwhile, heat the oil in a skillet over high heat. Add the meatballs and fry until browned on all sides and cooked, about 5 minutes. Shake the pan as you are doing so to prevent the meatballs from sticking to the pan.

Season the soup with salt, pepper, cayenne pepper and lemon juice, then add the meatballs. Chop the chervil and remaining parsley. Serve the soup piping hot, sprinkled with the herbs.

1   **Preparing the onion.** Press the cloves into the onion. Make a slit in one side of the onion with a sharp knife and press the bay leaf firmly into it. Add to the stock with herbs and chopped vegetables.

2   **Rolling the meatballs in flour.** Place the flour in a shallow dish and roll the meatballs carefully in it. Put them aside for a few moments to allow the flour to dry.

3   **Thickening the soup.** Stir the fried bread crumbs and garlic mixture into the boiling stock. Reduce the heat and simmer for 5 minutes, stirring frequently.

Our tip

As with all soups, the quality of the stock is of decisive importance for the flavor and consistency of barcelonessa. The meat, with or without bone, is first placed in cold water and brought very slowly to a boil. During this process a layer of thick gray scum will form on the surface. This must be skimmed off frequently until the stock clears or until the foam becomes fine and white in appearance. During the whole cooking process the stock must not be allowed to boil otherwise the scum will not settle on the surface and, as a result, the stock will not be clear. Should the stock begin to boil, add a little cold water so that the temperature drops below boiling point. The scum should then slowly rise to the surface again.

Shrimp Bisque

The preparation of crayfish bisque requires a good deal of time, but it is well worth the effort. Virtually no other soup tastes so exquisitely delicious. If crayfish are not available, 2 lb shrimps may be substituted.

Serves 8

---

16 crayfish, fresh or cooked,
each weighing about 2 oz
1 bunch fresh dill
6 quarts water
1½ tablespoons salt
2 carrots
2 shallots
1 small onion
2 sprigs fresh thyme
3 sprigs fresh parsley
6 tablespoons butter
¼ cup brandy
2½ cups dry white wine
1 bay leaf
3 tablespoons flour
2 cups light cream
freshly ground white pepper
cayenne pepper

Preparation time: 2½ hours
Cooling time: about 2 hours

If you have been able to obtain fresh, uncooked crayfish, scrub them thoroughly under cold running water. Rinse the dill and put a little aside for use as a garnish later. Put the rest of the dill in a very large saucepan with the water and salt and bring to a boil. Boil for 5 minutes so that the pan is thoroughly hot; the addition of the crayfish should not reduce the water temperature. Add the crayfish to the fiercely boiling water and continue to boil for 1 minute, then reduce the heat and simmer for a further 5 minutes. Remove the pan from the heat and put aside to allow the crayfish and stock to cool. This will take about 2 hours.

Peel the carrots, shallots and onion and chop very finely. Rinse the thyme and parsley under cold running water, shake dry and chop coarsely.

Remove the crayfish from the stock and twist off the tails. Pick the meat from the tail shells and remove the intestinal vein. This looks like a black thread and is found on the back of the tail meat. It can be easily removed with a sharp knife. Put the shells to one side together with the legs which should also be removed. Break open the claws by twisting the smaller half of each at the joint and cracking open the larger half. Remove the meat without separating the two halves of the claw. Put aside a few of the better claws and a few whole pieces of tail meat to use as a garnish. Pound the rest of the meat to a fine paste in a mortar and pestle or food processor and put aside.

Divide the shells into portions and pound each portion in a mortar with a pestle, or grind to a pulp in a blender or food processor, adding a little stock if necessary. Heat 3 tablespoons of the butter in a heavy skillet. Add the vegetables, herbs and crushed shell. Heat, stirring occasionally, until the mixture begins to take on color. Add the warmed brandy and ignite. Let it burn for a few seconds before quenching the flames with half of the wine. Add the bay leaf and cook for a further 10 minutes, then pass the mixture through a fine sieve.

Melt 2 tablespoons of the butter in a saucepan. Stir in the flour until it has been absorbed then add the rest of the wine, the sieved shell purée and the crayfish meat paste. Stir in the cream and cook for 5–10 minutes or until the liquid has reduced a little and acquired a creamy consistency.

Remove the pan from the heat. Cut the remaining butter into small pieces and whisk them into the soup. Season to taste with salt, pepper and cayenne pepper and serve immediately, garnished with the few whole pieces of crayfish meat and claws that were set aside and the rest of the dill.

1 **Cooking the crayfish.** If dealing with live crayfish, grip each firmly by the back and place head first in the boiling water, pressing it immediately under the surface.

2 **Removing the meat.** Twist off the tails and pick the meat from the shells. Remove the intestinal vein, the black thread found on the back of the tail meat.

3 **Breaking open the claws.** Twist the smaller half of the claw at the joint and break open the larger half. Remove the meat so that the two claws halves are not separated.

4 **Pounding the shells.** Reduce the shells to a pulp in small portions using a mortar and pestle, or a blender or food processor.

Our tip

The shells must be thoroughly pounded in order to release their full aroma; for this you can use a pestle and mortar or a blender or food processor. Whatever is used, the job will be made easier if the shells are first broken or crushed with a cleaver or large kitchen knife.

Paella

The ingredients for this Spanish stew may be varied according to budget and season, but always include meat, poultry, shell-fish, vegetables and rice.

Serves 6

1–1½ dozen fresh mussels
6 tablespoons dry white wine
or water
½ lb green beans
salt
8 jumbo shrimp, fresh or frozen
(about ¾ lb)
1 small roaster chicken (1¾ lb)
5 oz pork tenderloin · 2 onions
3–4 cloves garlic · 1 sweet red pepper
2 large ripe tomatoes
6–8 tablespoons olive oil
freshly ground black pepper
1½ cups rice
3¾ cups boiling water
¼ teaspoon crumbled saffron threads
½ lb chorizo sausage
1 cup frozen peas
8 stuffed green olives
lemon quarters for garnish
(optional)

Preparation time: 1¼ hours

Scrub and clean the mussel shells thoroughly in several changes of cold water; discard any which are already open. Remove the beards. Cook the mussels in the wine or water in a large wide pan for 5 minutes, then remove from the shells. Discard any mussels that have not opened. Strain the stock and reserve.

Trim the beans and break into 1 inch lengths. Parboil the beans in salted water for 3–4 minutes, then drain in a colander and refresh under cold running water. If using frozen shrimp, thaw them first and pat dry with paper towels. Cut the chicken into eight pieces, wipe the pieces with a damp cloth and pat dry. Cut the pork into ½ inch cubes. Peel and chop the onions and garlic. Halve the red pepper, remove the core and seeds, and cut into strips about ¼ inch side. Scald the tomatoes in boiling water for 10 seconds then peel, remove the core and discard the seeds. Chop the flesh finely.

Preheat the oven to 400°F. Heat 3 tablespoons of the oil in a paella pan or

shallow flameproof casserole. Season the chicken pieces with salt and pepper, add them to the pan and brown well on all sides. Remove the chicken. Add the shrimp and fry for a few minutes. Remove the shrimp and discard the oil. Heat the remaining oil (3–5 tablespoons) in the pan until it is hot. Brown the pork cubes and remove, then fry the onions, garlic and red pepper gently until they are soft. Add the chopped tomatoes and cook briskly until the juices in the pan have been substantially reduced.

Rinse the rice in a sieve, shake dry and place in the pan with the vegetables. Cook for a few minutes, stirring well, before adding the boiling water and the reserved mussel stock. When the rice becomes translucent, season with salt, pepper and saffron and bring to a boil, stirring constantly. Remove from the heat.

Slice the chorizo and place in the pan together with the chicken pieces, pork cubes, shrimp and beans. Stir the frozen peas under the other ingredients; they should be completely covered with liquid. Place the pan in the heated oven and cook for about 30 minutes or until the rice is tender. Stir in the sliced olives and the mussels 5 minutes before the end of cooking. Serve immediately, garnished with lemon quarters if desired.

Our tip

Do as the Spaniards do and cook the paella over an open wood or charcoal fire at your next barbecue. Follow the recipe but increase the amount of liquid – more will evaporate when it is prepared in the open. Stir the paella frequently during the cooking process so that the ingredients cook evenly and the rice on the surface does not become hard and dry. Paella is traditionally served straight out of the pan, with a fresh salad of tomatoes, mild onions and lettuce served separately. Spanish wine goes best with paella, of course, although a domestic wine makes an acceptable alternative.

1 **Adding the tomatoes.** Add the chopped tomatoes to the vegetables in the pan and, stirring briskly, cook over a fierce heat in order to reduce any liquid from the vegetables.

2 **Seasoning the rice.** Season the rice with salt, pepper and saffron when it has become glassy in appearance. Bring to a boil, stirring constantly, then remove from the heat.

3 **Adding the peas.** Make sure that the frozen peas are well covered with liquid otherwise they will dry out during the cooking process. Place in the heated oven and complete the cooking.

Chilli con Carne

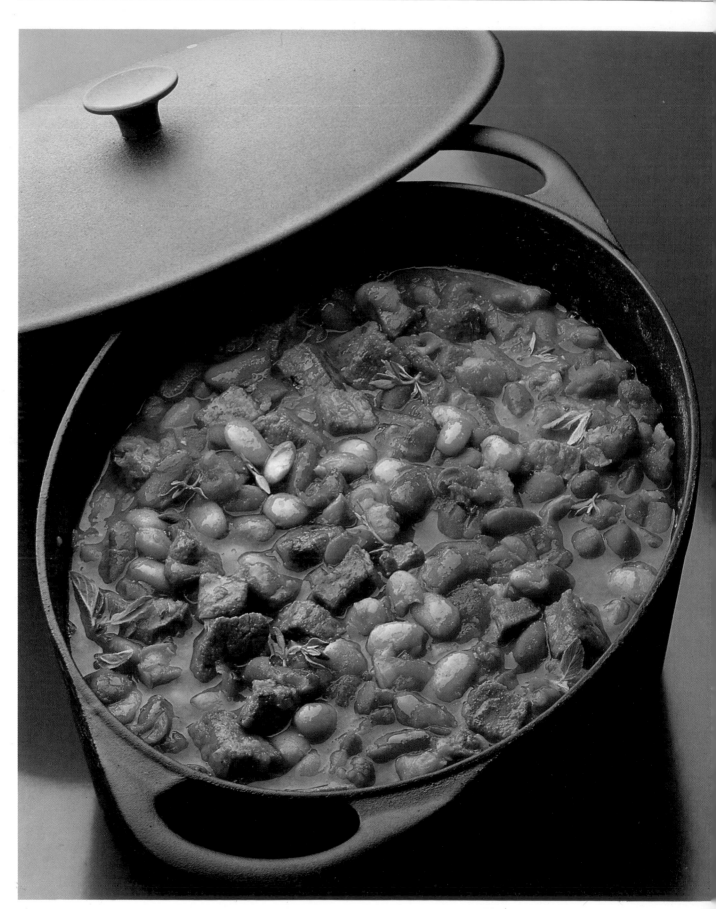

Very hot, very sharp and very substantial - that is how chili con carne, the fiery Mexican stew, should be. It is just the thing to serve at an informal party. If you cannot get the beans mentioned in the recipe, you can of course use other dried beans (white, brown or black). Do not, however, add the salt or the tomatoes earlier than mentioned in the recipe since both prolong the cooking time of beans.

Serves 12

4 cups dried red kidney beans
4 cups dried pinto beans
6 quarts water
8 onions
6–7 cloves garlic
4½ lb beef for stew
6 tablespoons olive oil
4–5 chili peppers (fresh or dried)
3–4 sprigs fresh or
½ teaspoon dried oregano
3–4 sprigs fresh or
½ teaspoon dried thyme
2 sprigs fresh or
½ teaspoon dried sage
2 tablespoons sweet paprika
½ teaspoon cayenne pepper
3 lb tomatoes

Soaking time: 12–24 hours
Preparation time: 2¼ hours

Rinse and drain the beans. Place them in a large saucepan with the cold water and leave them to soak overnight. On the following day, bring the soaking water and beans quickly to a boil. Continue to cook over a moderate heat for 30 minutes.

Peel the onions and chop them finely. Peel and chop the garlic. Cut the meat into ¾ inch cubes. Heat about half of the oil in a large, heavy-based saucepan and fry the meat, a few pieces at a time, until it is well browned on all sides. Remove each portion as it is browned and place in a metal sieve with a dish underneath to catch any juices. Add more oil to the pan if necessary. As soon as all the meat has been browned, heat the oil in the pan once more and place all the meat in it, without the meat juices. Cook, turning, for a few more minutes until really brown and crisp.

Push the meat to one side of the pan and fry the onions, stirring frequently, until they are soft and golden. Then add the garlic and cook for 2–3 minutes, taking care that it does not burn. Add the beans and the liquid in which they were cooked. You can do this by carefully pouring them from one pan into the other or by using a large ladle. The ladle method avoids the dangers of splashes of hot liquid and steam.

Cut open the chili peppers and remove the seeds. Rinse, pat dry and cut them across into rings. Dried chili peppers should be lightly crumbled. Rinse the herbs and shake dry. Place in the stew with the chili peppers. Season with paprika and cayenne pepper. Add the meat juices, cover the pan and simmer gently for 1 hour.

Meanwhile scald the tomatoes in boiling water for 10 seconds, then peel and remove the core and any hard green stem. Cut the tomatoes in half so all seed chambers are visible and, taking half a tomato at a time in the palm of your hand, squeeze gently until the seeds fall out. Discard these, chop the flesh coarsely and add to the stew with salt to taste. Cook for a further 15 minutes, then season to taste with pepper and more cayenne pepper if desired. Serve very hot.

1 Chopping the onions. Cut the onions in half lengthwise. Slice each half parallel to the work surface. Then slice lengthwise vertically and then across into even dice.

2 Frying the onions. Push the meat to one side of the pan and, stirring frequently, cook the onions until they are soft and golden. Then add the garlic.

3 Adding the beans. Pour the beans and the liquid directly from one pan into the other, or transfer them with a ladle to avoid danger of splashes of hot liquid.

Clam Chowder

Here in North America this creamy shellfish soup is usually served with unsalted crackers.

Serves 8

1½–2 dozen fresh mussels
1½–2 dozen fresh clams
2 onions
2 carrots
2 stalks celery, or ¼ celeriac
2 bunches fresh parsley
6 tablespoons dry white wine
about 6 tablespoons water
salt
freshly ground white pepper
3 oz slab bacon
2 small green peppers
¾ lb potatoes
2 sprigs fresh or
½ teaspoon dried thyme
2 large ripe tomatoes
1 tablespoon butter or oil
1 tablespoon flour
6 tablespoons hot chicken broth
6 tablespoons hot milk
¾ cup light cream
pinch sweet paprika
1 sprig fresh dill

Preparation time: 1 hour

Scrub and clean the shellfish thoroughly in several changes of cold water. Discard any which are already open. Remove the beards from mussels by holding firmly between thumb and knife blade and scraping them off. Place the shellfish in a large pan.

Peel and finely chop the onions and carrots. Trim the celery and slice, or peel and dice the celeriac. Put half the bunch of parsley aside and coarsely chop the remainder.

Put the carrots, celery or celeriac, half the onions and the chopped parsley in the pan with the shellfish. Pour in the wine and sufficient water so that the shellfish are just covered. Add a little salt and a generous amount of pepper. Cover the pan and quickly bring to a boil. Shake the pan frequently so that all the shellfish get an equal amount of heat. Boil for about 5 minutes or until all the shells have opened. Remove the shellfish and discard any that are still shut. Strain the stock through a paper coffee filter or through a fine sieve lined with a damp cloth. Set aside.

Chop the bacon finely. Halve the green peppers, remove the seeds and core, and cut into fine dice. Peel and dice the potatoes. Rinse the thyme and shake dry. Put aside one sprig of the remaining parsley and chop the rest finely with the thyme. Scald the tomatoes in boiling water for 10 seconds, then peel and remove the core and any pieces of hard stem. Cut the tomatoes in half and, taking half a tomato in the palm of your hand, squeeze until the seeds fall out. Discard these and chop the flesh.

Fry the bacon gently in a large pan until the fat begins to run. Add the butter or oil and fry the remaining onion and the green peppers until they are soft. Sprinkle the flour over the ingredients in the pan stir in and cook until it becomes golden and frothy. Mix together the chicken broth, shellfish stock and milk and add to the pan, stirring constantly. Bring to a boil, stirring. Add the potatoes, chopped herbs and tomatoes and simmer for 15 minutes. Stir in the cream and simmer until the liquid has reduced and the soup has acquired a creamy consistency.

Remove the mussels and clams from their shells and chop about three-quarters of them. Place the chopped and whole shellfish in the soup and heat through gently. Season with paprika and garnish with the dill and reserved parsley sprig before serving.

1 **Straining the stock.** In order to remove any sand, strain the stock through a paper coffee filter or through a fine sieve lined with a damp cloth.

2 **Adding the flour.** When the bacon, onions and green peppers are soft, sprinkle the flour over them and stir until the liquid becomes golden and frothy.

3 **Adding the liquid.** Mix the shellfish stock with the chicken broth and the milk and pour slowly over the vegetables, stirring constantly until it comes to a boil.

Our tip

The best times for fresh shellfish are the months with an "r" in them – September to April. Discard any that are not tightly shut or do not shut immediately when given a sharp tap. Shellfish that are open are usually dead and therefore poisonous. The same rule applies to shellfish that do not open during the cooking process: they should also be discarded. You can prepare clam chowder with canned or bottled shellfish if fresh shellfish is not available. However, it is essential to use shellfish in brine as that preserved in a marinade is too strong in flavor.

Ratatouille with Lamb

This combination of lamb, vegetables and fresh herbs stewed together in their own juices produces a beautifully aromatic dish.

Serves 4

2 large ripe tomatoes
2 cloves garlic
2 onions
1 sweet red pepper
1 green pepper
2 small eggplants
2 medium-sized zucchini
$\frac{1}{2}$ small leek
1–2 stalks celery
1 lb lean boneless lamb
(from the leg)
6 tablespoons olive oil
salt
freshly ground black pepper
2 sprigs fresh or
$\frac{1}{2}$ teaspoon dried rosemary
2 sprigs fresh or
$\frac{1}{2}$ teaspoon dried thyme
1 bunch fresh or
2 teaspoons dried parsley
1 bunch fresh basil or
1 teaspoon dried
1 bay leaf

Preparation time: $1\frac{1}{4}$ hours

Scald the tomatoes in boiling water for 10 seconds, then remove the skins and any hard pieces of core. Cut the tomatoes in half so that all the seed chambers are visible and, taking half a tomato at a time in the palm of your hand, squeeze gently until the seeds fall out. Discard the seeds and chop the flesh.

Peel the garlic and onions. Chop the garlic finely and slice the onions. Halve the red and green peppers, remove the core and seeds and chop into fairly large pieces. Rinse and dry the eggplants and zucchini. Remove the stalks and cut into halves or quarters lengthwise, then slice crosswise. Trim the leek and celery and slice both thinly. Place the leek in a sieve and rinse to remove any soil that might remain. Cut the lamb into $\frac{3}{4}$ inch cubes.

Preheat the oven to 400°F. Heat the oil in a wide flameproof casserole and brown the meat, a few pieces at a time. When each portion is well browned, remove from the pan and place in a metal sieve with a dish underneath to catch the meat juices. When all the meat is browned, add the onions to the casserole and fry in the same fat until softened. Remove the onions with a slotted spoon and continue frying the vegetables, one after the other: first the peppers, then the eggplant, the zucchini and finally, the leek and celery with the garlic.

Put all the fried vegetables back in the casserole with the meat and add the tomatoes and the meat juices. Season to taste with salt and pepper. Rinse the herbs and shake dry. If using fresh basil, set half aside and chop the rest of the herbs finely. Stir into the ingredients in the casserole and place the bay leaf on top. Cover the casserole and place it in the heated oven. Cook for 45 minutes. Taste and adjust the seasoning, discard the bay leaf and serve garnished with the rest of the fresh basil.

Our tip

In Provence, ratatouille is more often served without meat as a vegetable stew, and it makes a refreshingly light and tasty summer or autumn dish that can be served hot or cold. If served cold, it must be seasoned again before serving as the intensity of the seasoning diminishes during the cooling process. Composed entirely of vegetables, ratatouille makes an excellent accompaniment for broiled or fried meat or can be served cold as an appetizer. Cold ratatouille can be garnished with basil as well.

1 **Removing the seeds from the tomatoes.** Cut the tomatoes in half so that all the seed chambers are visible. Squeeze gently so that the seeds fall out, and discard the seeds.

2 **Cut the meat into small cubes.** Heat the oil in a flameproof casserole and brown the cubes of meat well, adding them in batches to avoid crowding the pan.

3 **Mix the meat with the vegetables** and pour the meat juices back into the casserole with the tomatoes. Season with salt and pepper to taste, add the herbs and continue cooking in the oven.

German Beef and Vegetable Soup

This hearty variation of German vegetable soup contains generous amounts of beef, bacon and herbs in addition to a wide selection of vegetables.

Serves 8

1 ham hock
1 lb beef for stew
2 quarts water
1 bay leaf
4 carrots
½ celeriac
1 leek
1 bunch fresh parsley
2 sprigs fresh marjoram
2 lb potatoes
salt
freshly ground black pepper
grated nutmeg
6 scallions
1 cup mushrooms
¼ lb slab bacon

Preparation time: 2 hours

Place the ham hock in a large saucepan with the water and bring slowly to a boil. When the stock is boiling, add the beef and the bay leaf and return to a boil. Skim off any gray scum which rises to the surface. It will be necessary to skim a number of times. Partially cover the pan and simmer gently for 1¼ hours. Check occasionally to see if any more scum has accumulated on the surface and skim off. While the stock is simmering, prepare the vegetables.

Peel or scrape the carrots and cut into neat dice. Pluck any leaves from the celeriac, rinse and shake dry. Peel the celeriac and chop into neat dice. Trim the leek and slice into ¼ inch rings. Place in a sieve and rinse to remove any soil which might remain. Rinse the herbs, shake dry and chop finely together with the celeriac leaves, if any. Peel the potatoes and cut into ½ inch cubes.

Place the vegetables in the stock and season to taste with salt, pepper and nutmeg. Continue to simmer for a further 30 minutes. Just before the end of cooking time, trim the scallions. Cut the white part of the scallions into small dice and the green stalks into neat rings. Clean the mushrooms and slice as thinly as possible. Cut the bacon into tiny cubes. Fry the bacon gently in a skillet until the fat is rendered. Add the scallions and fry, stirring occasionally, until golden. Add the mushrooms and fry briefly. Drain the mixture on paper towels and set aside.

Remove the beef and ham hock from the soup. Discard the ham hock. Place the beef in a sieve so that any stock runs off. Remove any fat or gristle and cut the beef into meat pieces.

Remove about one-third of the vegetables from the soup, mash vegetables with a fork, and put back into the soup together with the beef. The mashed vegetables give the soup a thicker consistency. Stir the soup well to distribute the beef. Taste and adjust the seasoning, and discard the bay leaf. Add the bacon and mushroom mixture and serve immediately.

1 **Preparing the carrots.** Peel or scrape the carrots and trim off the ends, then cut lengthwise into strips of equal size and finally into small cubes, using a sharp knife.

2 **Dicing the potatoes.** Peel the potatoes. Cut into slices $\frac{1}{4}$ inch thick. Lay the slices on top of one another, cut into strips and then across into $\frac{1}{2}$ inch cubes.

3 **Preparing the meat.** Place the cooked beef in a sieve to drain off any stock, then carefully remove any fat or gristle and cut the meat into neat pieces. Return to the soup with the mashed vegetables.

Our tip

If you cannot obtain a ham hock, double the quantity of beef and include a beef bone. Add a thick piece of bacon rind, if available, to the stock to enhance the flavor.

Bigos

Bigos is a Polish national dish: a hunter's stew. Cook it slowly so that the flavors of the various meat and vegetables blend well together.

Serves 6

1 lb beef for stew
½ lb veal for stew
½ lb pork for stew
5 oz salami, in one piece
1 cup mushrooms
½ small head white cabbage
1 apple
2 onions
1 large tomato
2 tablespoons butter
1 lb sauerkraut
2 tablespoons vegetable oil
5 tablespoons Madeira or white wine
1 cup chicken or beef broth
1–2 sprigs fresh or ¼ teaspoon dried marjoram
2 cloves garlic
pinch cumin seeds
2 whole or ¼ teaspoon ground allspice
1 bay leaf
salt
freshly ground black pepper

Preparation time: 2 hours

Cut meats into 1 inch cubes, keeping each kind of meat separate. Roughly chop the salami. Clean the mushrooms and halve any large ones. Remove dry coarse outer leaves from the cabbage. Cut the cabbage in half, remove the core, rinse, drain and shred finely. Peel and core the apple, slice thinly lengthwise and then once crosswise. Peel and chop the onions. Scald the tomato in boiling water for 10 seconds and peel. Remove the core and any hard stem. Cut the tomato in half so that all seed chambers are visible and, taking half a tomato at a time in the palm of your hand, squeeze gently until the seeds fall out. Discard, and chop the flesh coarsely.

Preheat the oven to 400°F. Melt half the butter in a flameproof casserole and fry the apple and onions until lightly browned, turning frequently. Drain the sauerkraut, if liked, and break it up with a fork. Place in the casserole together with the mushrooms, cabbage and tomato. Continue to cook over a moderate heat for 5 minutes, stirring occasionally, then remove from the heat and set aside.

Heat a little of the oil and remaining butter in a skillet. Fry each kind of meat separately, finishing with the pieces of salami, until well browned on all sides. Add more oil and butter as necessary. As soon as each batch of meat is browned, place it in the casserole on top of the vegetables so that any meat juices run over the vegetables. When all the meat is in the casserole, mix the vegetables and the meat together.

Heat any fat or juices remaining in the skillet and add the wine and broth. Bring to a boil, stirring constantly with a wooden spoon to loosen any sediment sticking to the pan. Boil to reduce the liquid.

Meanwhile rinse and shake dry the marjoram. Tear the leaves into small pieces. Peel and chop the garlic. Add the marjoram, garlic, cumin seeds, allspice and bay leaf to the casserole and season to taste with salt and pepper. Gradually pour the reduced liquid over the meat and vegetables, shaking the casserole from time to time so that the liquid is well distributed. Cover the casserole and place in the heated oven. Cook for 1½ hours or until all the meats are tender. Taste and adjust the seasoning, and discard the bay leaf before serving.

1 **Placing the meat on the vegetables.** Place each batch of browned meat on top of the vegetables as soon as it is done so that any meat juices blend with the vegetables.

2 **Loosening the meat sediments.** Heat the fat again and add the wine and broth. Stir to loosen any sediment and then boil to reduce the liquid.

3 **Adding the liquid.** Pour the mixture of wine, broth and meat juices over the vegetables slowly, shaking the casserole occasionally so that the liquid becomes well distributed.

Borsch

Whether you serve borscht as a main dish or as a little snack during an informal party (in which case this recipe will be enough for six), this hearty beet soup based on the Russian original will always find enthusiastic takers. Serve it with wholewheat, rye or black bread.

Serves 6

2 lb lean beef for stew
2 small marrow bones
2½ quarts water
3 onions · 4 carrots
1 leek · 1 stalk celery
5–6 sprigs fresh parsley
2 bay leaves
1 lb fresh beets,
uncooked
½ celeriac · 2 cloves garlic
3 tablespoons butter
½ teaspoon sugar
¼ cup red wine vinegar
½ small head cabbage or
½ lb tomatoes
salt · ¼ lb cooked ham
2 frankfurters
freshly ground black pepper
5–6 sprigs fresh dill
¾ cup sour cream

Preparation time: 3½ hours

Place the beef and the bones in a large saucepan. Add the cold water and bring to a boil over a gentle heat. Reduce the heat and remove any gray scum which has risen to the surface with a skimming spoon. This must be done several times to produce a clear stock. The stock should now simmer very gently; never allow it to boil or the scum will not rise and settle.

Meanwhile, peel two of the onions and two of the carrots. Trim and wash the leek and celery. Coarsely chop these vegetables. Rinse the parsley, shake dry and chop. Place the vegetables, parsley and bay leaves in the stock and turn up the heat to bring it back to simmering point. When the stock begins to simmer, reduce the heat a little, partially cover the pan and cook very gently for a further 1 hour.

Remove the beef and place to one side. Continue to simmer the stock and vegetables for a further 1 hour. The pan should only be partially covered so that the stock gradually reduces to about 1 quart. Then strain the stock and remove as much fat as possible.

Peel and chop the remaining onion. Peel or scrape the remaining carrots, the beets and celeriac and cut into small strips about the size of matchsticks. Peel the garlic and chop finely or crush. Melt the butter in a large saucepan and fry the onion until it is soft. Add the carrots, beets, celeriac and garlic and fry gently for a few minutes. Add the sugar and the vinegar. Pour in a little stock and bring to a boil, then reduce to a simmer.

Remove any coarse outer leaves from the cabbage, cut it in half, remove the core, rinse, drain and shred finely. Scald the tomatoes in boiling water for 10 seconds and peel. Remove the core. Cut the tomatoes in half so that all seed chambers are visible and, taking half a tomato at a time, in the palm of your hand, squeeze gently to remove the seeds. Discard the seeds, chop the flesh coarsely and place in the saucepan with the cabbage. Season with salt, add the rest of the stock and simmer for 30 minutes.

Remove any fat from the beef. Cut the ham, frankfurters and beef into strips about ¼ inch wide. Place in the soup, season and continue to simmer for a further 30 minutes. Rinse the dill and shake dry. Adjust the seasoning, and pour into a large heated soup tureen. Pour the sour cream into the center and serve, garnished with the dill.

1 Skimming the stock. Remove the gray scum which keeps forming on the surface of the stock, using a skimming spoon, so that the stock becomes as clear as possible.

2 Preparing the cabbage. Remove any coarse outer leaves, cut the cabbage in half and cut out the stalk with a sharp knife. Rinse and drain the cabbage, then shred finely.

3 Adding the meat. Place the strips of beef, ham and frankfurter in the stock with the vegetables. Season lightly with salt, but add a generous amount of black pepper.

Our tip

Fresh beets are available from October to May. If possible, buy them with the leaves or stalk still attached. If all the stalks have been removed, they will bleed and lose most of their flavor. It is possible to freeze borscht; in fact, it freezes admirably. Prepare it as described in the recipe but use slightly less seasoning and reduce the cooking time. When it has cooled, pack it into containers and freeze. Before using, place the borscht in a saucepan with a little water and heat gently until thawed. Bring to a boil, season to taste and serve with the sour cream and dill.

Avocado Salad

Ripe avocados and smoked beef or ham give this salad a slightly nutty aroma that harmonizes well with crisp lettuce and hearts of palm.

Serves 4

---

1 (16-oz) can hearts of palm
½ head iceberg lettuce
1 cup button mushrooms
juice of 1½ lemons
2 ripe avocados
(each weighing about ½ lb)
¾ cup plain yogurt
salt
freshly ground white pepper
pinch sugar · pinch cayenne pepper
few drops Worcestershire sauce
1–2 tablespoons gin
1 teaspoon nut oil
2 oz smoked beef or ham
(prosciutto), sliced very thinly
several sprigs watercress

Preparation time: 45 minutes

Drain the hearts of palm and cut them diagonally into slices ½ inch wide. Rinse the lettuce thoroughly in cold water and shake dry in a salad basket or dish towel. Tear the leaves into small pieces. Clean the mushrooms and cut off the base of the stalks. Slice the mushrooms very thinly and sprinkle with lemon juice to prevent them going brown.

Cut the avocados in half by slicing them lengthwise around the seed and twisting the two halves apart. Brush the cut surfaces at once with lemon juice to prevent discoloration. Score the avocado skins lengthwise with a sharp knife and pull off the skin in strips. Brush the exposed surfaces with lemon juice. Put half an avocado aside for the dressing and cut the rest crosswise into slices ¼ inch thick. Sprinkle with lemon juice again.

Mash the reserved avocado half and pass through a plastic sieve if necessary to make the purée smooth (the sieve used should on no account be made of metal which would cause the avocado to discolor). Mix the avocado purée with the yogurt and the rest of the lemon juice, and season to taste with salt, pepper, sugar, cayenne and Worcestershire sauce. Beat the gin and nut oil into the dressing drop by drop and season again if necessary; the dressing should be piquant in flavor.

Arrange the lettuce, avocado slices, palm hearts and mushrooms on a large salad plate or as individual portions on smaller plates. Loosely roll the beef or ham slices and arrange them around the edges of the salad. Place the dressing on top of the salad; do not mix it with the ingredients. Rinse the watercress under cold running water, shake dry and chop finely. Sprinkle over the salad as a garnish and serve immediately.

1 **Halve the avocados** by cutting them lengthwise around the seed and twisting the two halves apart. Do this gently to avoid bruising the avocado flesh.

2 **Peeling the avocados.** Score the skins lengthwise with a sharp knife and strip off the skin. Brush the surface of the fruit with lemon juice to prevent discoloration.

3 **Cleaning the mushrooms.** Trim the stalks and wipe the tops with a damp cloth. Slice very thinly and sprinkle with lemon juice to prevent them from turning brown.

4 **Preparing the dressing.** Mix the avocado purée, yogurt, the rest of the lemon juice and the seasonings together. Beat in the gin and nut oil very gradually and season again to make sure that the dressing is piquant enough.

Our tip

Only use ripe avocados for this salad as only ripe fruit has that delicate nutty flavor that goes so well with the other ingredients. Gently squeeze the fruit in the palm of your hand to test for ripeness. It will give a little if it is ripe. If only hard avocados are available, buy them a few days beforehand, wrap them in newspaper and leave them to ripen in a warm place.

Salade Nouvelle with Goose Liver

If you wish to eat as well at home as you would in an exclusive restaurant, try this nouvelle cuisine recipe for a salad with fried goose liver slices. Serve it simply with fresh French bread and a glass of white port or medium dry sherry.

Serves 4

$\frac{1}{4}$ lb green beans
salt
handful chicory leaves
4 leaves radicchio (red lettuce)
12 leaves young spinach
$\frac{1}{2}$ large ripe tomato
8 button mushrooms
juice of $\frac{1}{2}$ lemon
small pinch sugar
freshly ground white pepper
1–2 teaspoons sherry vinegar
1 teaspoon raspberry or
other fruit vinegar
2 tablespoons olive oil
1 teaspoon hazelnut or
walnut oil
1$\frac{1}{2}$ tablespoons white port or
medium dry sherry
$\frac{1}{2}$ canned truffle (optional)
$\frac{1}{2}$ lb fresh goose liver or
canned pâté de foie gras

Preparation time: 30 minutes

Trim the beans and break them into pieces about 1$\frac{1}{2}$ inches in length. Cook them in boiling salted water for 3–4 minutes, then drain in a colander. They should be just tender but still crisp. Pour ice cold water over them to refresh them, then put aside to drain and cool.

Rinse the chicory, radicchio and spinach leaves very thoroughly under cold running water. Dry them in a salad basket or with a clean dish towel. Scald the tomato in boiling water for 10 seconds, then peel, remove any core or hard green stem and cut the tomato in half. Take the tomato half in the palm of your hand and squeeze gently until the seeds fall out, then discard them. Slice the tomato into thin strips. Clean the mushrooms. Slice them very finely and sprinkle with lemon juice.

To make the dressing, mix together $\frac{1}{8}$ teaspoon of salt, the sugar and a little pepper with the sherry and fruit vinegars. Beat in the olive and nut oil gradually, then add the port or sherry and a few drops of liquid from the truffle can, if available.

Drain the truffle of any excess liquid and cut it first into thin slices and then into very fine strips. Scrape or peel the skin from the fresh liver, then cut it into slices about $\frac{1}{2}$ inch thick. Heat a skillet and without using any fat, fry the liver slices on both sides, allowing about 30 seconds for each side. Remove from the pan immediately and place on paper towels to drain off any excess fat. If you are using canned pâté, it should be sliced but not fried.

Toss each salad ingredient separately in the dressing and arrange with the slices of liver and the truffle strips on four dinner plates. As in the illustration, the dish should not only be a delicacy for the palate but a pleasure for the eye as well.

1 **Drying the salad.** Place the rinsed spinach, radicchio and chicory leaves in a clean dish towel or salad basket and shake them to remove excess liquid.

2 **Preparing the mushrooms.** Clean the mushrooms and slice very thinly. Sprinkle them with the juice of half a lemon to prevent them turning brown.

3 **Preparing the truffle.** Drain the truffle of any excess liquid in the can and cut it into very thin slices with a sharp knife; then cut the slices into very thin strips.

4 **Removing the skin from the liver.** Take a sharp knife and scrape or peel off the skin. Cut the liver into slices about ½ inch thick. (Cut pâté into the same size slices.)

Our tip

Fresh goose livers are an expensive and hard-to-find delicacy. If they are not available, slices of canned pâté de foie gras may be used instead. The slices of pâté should not be fried.

Stuffed Peppers

Here are four different recipes for stuffed peppers which are all prepared in basically the same way; the preparation of the different fillings is a theme with variations, but the cooking of the stuffed peppers remains the same. The pepper at the back of the pan is stuffed with rice and turkey, on the right with lamb and rice, center front with a mixture of ground pork and beef and on the left with a mushroom and cheese filling.

Serves 4

4 peppers of about the same size
2 tablespoons oil · 2 tablespoons butter
6 tablespoons chicken broth
$\frac{1}{4}$ cup dry white wine
2 tablespoons heavy or
sour cream

For the rice and turkey stuffing:
$\frac{1}{2}$ cup long grain rice
3 tablespoons olive oil · 1 onion
10 oz turkey breast
2 large ripe tomatoes
3 tablespoons raisins
$\frac{1}{4}$ cup shelled pistachio nuts
salt · freshly ground white pepper
cayenne pepper · lemon juice
small bunch fresh parsley
1 sprig fresh thyme
$\frac{1}{4}$ teaspoon crumbled saffron threads
6 tablespoons hot chicken broth

Preparation time: 1$\frac{1}{2}$ hours

Prepare the peppers by cutting off the tops about $\frac{1}{2}$ inch below the stalk. Twist out the cores and cut out the inner ribs. Rinse under cold water, making sure that all the seeds have been removed, and pat dry.

To make the stuffing, heat the oil in a saucepan and fry the rice gently for 5 minutes or until it is translucent. Peel and finely chop the onion. Cut the turkey meat into tiny strips. Add both to the rice. Scald the tomatoes in boiling water for 10 seconds, then peel and remove the core and any piece of hard stem. Cut the tomatoes in half so that all seed chambers are visible and squeeze gently until the seeds fall out. Discard these and chop the flesh. Place the tomatoes, raisins and pistachio nuts in the pan and season to taste with salt, pepper, cayenne pepper

and lemon juice. Wash the parsley and thyme, shake dry and chop very finely. Stir into the other ingredients in the pan. Dissolve the saffron in the hot broth, then pour into the pan. Bring the broth quickly to a boil, stirring constantly, then reduce the heat and simmer gently until the rice has absorbed all the liquid and is almost tender.

Using a teaspoon, fill the peppers with the rice mixture, pressing it down lightly with the back of the spoon. Heat the oil and butter in a flameproof casserole and place the peppers in the fat. Put the tops on the peppers and pour the broth and wine into the casserole. Cover and simmer gently for 40 minutes or until tender. Remove the peppers and keep warm. Stir the cream into the liquid in the casserole and boil to reduce a little. Pour this sauce into a heated serving dish, place the peppers in the sauce and serve.

Lamb and Rice Stuffing. Cook $\frac{1}{2}$ cup long-grain rice in boiling salted water for 10 minutes, then drain in a sieve and rinse it under cold running water. Drain and put aside to cool. Peel 2 onions and 2 cloves of garlic and chop finely. Fry both gently in 1 tablespoon of olive oil until they are soft and golden. Set aside to cool.

Mix together 1 lb ground lamb, the onion, garlic and rice. Season generously with salt, black pepper and $\frac{1}{4}$ teaspoon of ground cinnamon. Rinse 3 sprigs of fresh mint, shake dry and chop finely. Stir into the mixture. Stuff and cook the peppers as described in the basic recipe.

Ground Meat Stuffing. Soften a stale roll in water, then squeeze out the excess water and crumble the roll into small pieces. Peel 1 onion and 1–2 cloves of garlic and chop both finely. Mix the bread, onion and garlic with 1 lb ground meat (preferably a mixture of beef and pork). Rinse, dry and chop a bunch of parsley. Stir it into the mixture with $\frac{1}{2}$–1 tablespoon green peppercorns. Season to taste with salt and black pepper and a dash each of Worcestershire and hot pepper sauces. Stuff and cook the peppers as described in the basic recipe.

Mushroom and Cheese Stuffing. Peel and chop 1 onion and 1 clove of garlic. Clean and chop $\frac{3}{4}$ lb mushrooms. Fry the onion, garlic and mushrooms in 2 tablespoons oil until soft and transparent. Add $\frac{1}{3}$ cup

long-grain rice and fry gently until all the oil has been absorbed. Scald 2 tomatoes in boiling water for 10 seconds, then peel and chop. Rinse, dry and chop a few sprigs of parsley. Add the tomatoes and parsley to the rice mixture with 6 tablespoons broth and 2 tablespoons lemon juice. Season to taste with salt and pepper and cook for 10 minutes or until the rice is almost cooked.

Meanwhile, rinse, dry and chop 3 sprigs of fresh basil. Grate $\frac{1}{3}$ cup Parmesan cheese. Add the basil and cheese to the rice mixture and combine thoroughly. Stuff and cook the peppers as described in the basic recipe.

1 **Preparing the peppers.** Cut off the tops of the peppers about $\frac{1}{2}$ inch below the stalk. Twist out the cores and cut out the inner ribs. Rinse to remove all seeds.

2 **Pouring in the broth.** Dissolve the saffron in the hot broth and pour over the rice, stirring the mixture all the time. Bring rapidly to a boil, then simmer gently.

3 **Filling the peppers.** Use a teaspoon to stuff the peppers and press the mixture down lightly with the back of the spoon. Heat the oil and butter in a flameproof casserole.

4 **Cooking the peppers.** Place the peppers in the hot fat and press the tops in place. Pour the broth and dry white wine into the casserole. Cover and simmer until tender.

Gratin Dauphinois

This famous French potato dish goes well with lamb and other broiled meats or can be eaten as a light meal accompanied by a mixed salad.

Serves 4

---

2 lb mature baking potatoes
1 clove garlic
$\frac{1}{4}$ cup butter
salt
freshly ground black pepper
grated nutmeg
$\frac{3}{4}$ cup shredded Gruyère or
Swiss cheese
3 cups heavy cream

Preparation time: $1\frac{1}{4}$ hours

Preheat the oven to 400°F. Peel the potatoes and cut into slices about $\frac{1}{8}$ inch thick. Lay the slices on paper towels and pat dry. Peel the garlic and cut in half. Rub a shallow baking dish with the cut sides of the garlic to give the dish a pleasant aroma, then discard the garlic. Butter the dish generously, using half the butter. Put the potatoes in layers in the dish so that they overlap one another and season each layer with salt, pepper and nutmeg. The potatoes should not be higher than $1-1\frac{1}{2}$ inches in the dish and there should be a gap of at least $\frac{1}{2}$ inch at the top so that the cream cannot boil over.

Sprinkle the cheese over the potatoes evenly. Pour over the cream, making sure that all the gaps are filled. The potatoes should be covered with cream – it may be necessary to increase the amount of cream if the dish is large. Dot the remaining butter over the potatoes. Place in the heated oven. Depending on the type of potato used, the dish will take 45–60 minutes to cook. Test with a fork after 45 minutes to see if the potatoes are tender. If the potatoes are ready and the surface is golden and crisp, the gratin can be served. If the surface gets too brown before the potatoes are cooked through, cover with foil.

1 **Rubbing the dish with garlic.** Rub a shallow baking dish with the cut sides of the garlic. This will give the cooked potatoes a pleasant aroma without a strong garlic flavor.

2 **Putting the potatoes in the dish.** Put the potato slices in the dish so that they overlap one another. Season each layer with salt, pepper and grated nutmeg.

3 **Pouring in the cream.** Pour the cream over the potatoes and shredded cheese so that any spaces between the potatoes are filled. The potatoes should be completely covered with cream.

Our tip

Instead of cream, a mixture of milk and heavy cream, or milk and light cream with beaten eggs, can be used. The quantity of cheese can also be increased or decreased according to taste. The potatoes used should be of a starchy variety and preferably of the same size so that the slices cook evenly.

Beet and Broccoli Creams

These delicious little molded vegetable creams served with a cool cream sauce make an admirable hors d'oeuvre or appetizer. They can also be served with meat instead of the usual vegetables but then, of course, without the cream sauce.

1 lb fresh broccoli
salt
$\frac{3}{4}$ lb beets
$\frac{1}{4}$ cup butter
2 cups heavy cream
butter for greasing dishes
2 eggs plus
2 egg whites
freshly ground white pepper
sugar
lemon juice

For the cream sauce:
2 tablespoons sour cream
$\frac{1}{4}$ cup heavy cream
1 tablespoon sherry vinegar
salt
freshly ground white pepper
1 shallot
small bunch chives

Preparation time: $1\frac{1}{2}$ hours

Discard any coarse stalks from the broccoli and divide the tiny florets – about $\frac{3}{4}$ pound should remain. Bring a large saucepan of salted water to a boil, add the broccoli and blanch for 3 minutes. Drain and plunge into ice cold water. Leave the broccoli in a sieve to drain and cool. Peel the beets and cut into thin slices.

Preheat the oven to 325°F. Heat half of the butter in one saucepan and the remaining butter in another. Place the broccoli in one pan and the beets in the other and fry gently, stirring frequently, until the vegetables become a little glassy in appearance. Add half of the cream to each pan and bring to a boil. Reduce the heat and cook gently for a further 10 minutes or until the vegetables are soft. The liquid should also have reduced a little.

Meanwhile, butter eight individual ovenproof molds or ramekins and place in the refrigerator.

The vegetables must now be reduced to a purée. Place the broccoli mixture in the bowl of a blender or food processor and add an egg and an egg white. Season to taste with salt, pepper, a pinch of sugar and a little lemon juice. Turn the machine to the highest speed and process until the mixture is light and frothy in consistency. Alternatively, sieve the broccoli mixture to a purée, then beat in the egg, egg white and seasonings.

Take half the molds out of the refrigerator and rub with butter again. Fill with the broccoli mixture. Purée the beet mixture with the remaining egg, egg white and seasonings, and fill the remaining molds in the same way.

Place a thick layer of brown paper or newspaper on the bottom of a large baking pan and stand the molds on the paper. Pour in enough hot water to come halfway up the sides of the molds. Bake in the heated oven for 55–60 minutes.

Meanwhile, prepare the cream sauce. Stir together the sour cream, heavy cream and sherry vinegar and season to taste with salt and pepper. Peel the shallot and chop it finely. Rinse the chives, shake dry and cut into very short lengths with scissors. Stir the shallot and chives into the sauce and place in the refrigerator to chill until it is served.

When the creams are ready, remove them from the pan of water. Run a sharp knife around the edges so that they do not stick and unmold them onto a heated serving plate or onto individual plates. Mop up any excess melted butter with paper towels. Pour a little of the sauce over each cream and serve immediately.

1 **Pouring in the cream.** As soon as the vegetables become slightly glassy, pour half the cream into each pan and bring to a boil. Cook gently for 10 minutes.

2 **Blending the vegetables.** Place the broccoli, the liquid in which it was cooked, an egg and an egg white in the blender or food processor. Season and purée.

3 **Placing the molds in the baking pan.** Put a thick layer of brown paper or newspaper on the bottom of the baking pan and stand the molds on it.

4 **Removing the creams.** Run a sharp knife around the edges of the creams to loosen them. Unmold onto a serving plate or individual plates. Pour a little sauce over each one and serve immediately.

Our tip

The molds or ramekins must be buttered generously so that the delicate vegetable creams do not stick to the sides when being unmolded onto the plates. Rub generously with softened butter and chill in the refrigerator so that the butter hardens before buttering again before use. This will ensure a smooth surface to the unmolded creams.

Stuffed Artichokes

Crisp on the outside and juicy on the inside – that is how these stuffed artichokes should be when you serve them, with a glass of chilled dry white or rosé wine. The artichoke leaves, with filling, should be pulled off and eaten with the fingers and the bottom, or heart, with a knife and fork.

Serves 4

4 large globe artichokes
juice 1–2 lemons
1 thick slice white bread
3–4 tablespoons milk
1 shallot
1 clove garlic
small bunch fresh parsley
3 anchovy fillets
1 slice lean cooked ham
$\frac{1}{4}$ cup grated Gruyère or Swiss cheese
salt
freshly ground white pepper
6 tablespoons olive oil
2 cups dry white wine

Preparation time: $1\frac{1}{2}$ hours

Preheat the oven to 350°F. Remove the stalks from the artichokes by bending the stalks back and forth until they break off, or cut off using a sharp knife. Remove the hard threads from the base at the same time. Neaten the base and edges with a sharp knife and brush the cut surfaces with lemon juice to prevent discoloration. Cut off the tops of the artichokes about one-third of the distance from the tip. Trim off any remaining pointed leaves with kitchen scissors. Brush the cut edges with lemon juice. Place the artichokes upside-down on the working surface and press a few times until the leaves start to bend. Pull apart the center leaves and scoop out the hairy "choke" using a spoon. Rub all around the cut surfaces of the artichokes with lemon juice once more and put aside.

Now make the stuffing. Remove the crust from the slice of bread. Pour milk over the bread and leave to soak for 5 minutes. Peel the shallot and garlic and chop finely. Rinse the parsley, shake it dry and chop. If the anchovy fillets are very salty, they should be soaked in cold water for a while or rinsed under cold running water. Pat dry, then crush or chop them. Cut the ham into tiny cubes (about $\frac{1}{8}$ inch). Squeeze the bread to remove excess milk and place in a bowl with the shallot, garlic, parsley, anchovies, ham and cheese. Mix to a smooth creamy paste. Season to taste with salt and pepper.

Stuff the artichokes, working from the

outer leaves towards the center. The leaves should be pliable enough to be pulled away from one another.

Heat 2 tablespoons of the oil in a shallow flameproof dish. Place the artichokes in the dish and sprinkle with the remaining oil. Pour the wine into the dish, cover and place in the heated oven. Bake for 40–60 minutes, basting frequently with the wine in the dish. The artichokes are ready when the bases are soft (test with a skewer). Then increase the oven temperature to 425°F and cook for a further 5 minutes or until the artichokes become crisp and brown. Serve hot.

1 Removing the stalk. Bend the stalk back and forth until it breaks and pull the threads out of the base at the same time. Neaten the base and edges with a sharp knife.

2 Opening the leaves. Place the artichokes upside down on the work surface and press them until the leaves begin to bend. Brush all over with lemon juice.

3 Filling the artichokes. Starting with the outer leaves, bend the leaves apart and stuff the spaces in between.

Home-made Spaghetti in Gorgonzola Cream

The fresh flavor of homemade pasta is incomparably better than anything a factory can produce and those who have made pasta once will find it is well worth making again.

Serves 4

3½ cups flour
4 eggs
2 tablespoons olive oil
salt
½ lb Gorgonzola cheese
1 tablespoon butter
1 cup light cream
freshly ground black pepper
2 sprigs fresh basil

Resting time for the dough:
about 1 hour
Preparation time: 1 hour

Sift the flour onto the work surface and make a hollow in the middle. Beat the eggs and the oil together, season with ⅛ teaspoon of salt and pour into the depression in the flour. Work the ingredients together. As soon as it is a soft ball, the pasta machine can be used for the hard task of kneading the dough.

Set the machine at the widest roller setting and roll the dough through the machine. Fold three times, then turn at a right angle and put the dough through the machine again. Dust with flour from time to time and repeat the process again and again until the dough is smooth and silky looking (eight to ten times is usually sufficient). Cover the dough and leave to rest for 30 minutes (this increases the elasticity of the dough).

Cut the dough into four portions. Knead each portion again, as in the first stage, meanwhile keeping the other portions covered so that they do not dry out.

Put all the dough together again and put it through the machine at the widest roller setting. Decrease the setting gradually, rolling the dough again and again until it is very thin. It is easier when two people do this job – one putting the dough through the machine and the other turning the handle, and both catching and holding the dough as it emerges at the other end.

When the dough is thin enough, change the setting on the machine to use the narrow groove cutting roller. Put the dough through the machine in portions and let the spaghetti noodles run over the back of the hand as they emerge. Drape them over an indoor washing line or a clean broomstick laid between two kitchen chairs and let them dry for 20 minutes.

To make the sauce, chop the cheese into small pieces and place in a heavy saucepan or top of a double boiler with the butter. Melt over a gentle heat, stirring all the time to prevent the cheese sticking or burning. As soon as the cheese has melted, stir in the cream. Grind a little pepper over the sauce. Keep it warm over hot water while boiling the noodles.

Bring 1 gallon of salted water to a boil in a large saucepan. Place the noodles in the boiling water and cook for 1 minute. Drain in a large sieve or colander, shaking well to remove excess water. Put the drained noodles into the cream sauce and toss and turn them gently with two forks so that all strands are coated with the sauce. Divide among four heated plates and grind a little pepper over each portion. Rinse the basil and shake dry. Garnish each portion of spaghetti with a few basil leaves and serve hot.

1 Kneading the dough. Roll the dough through the machine at the widest roller setting. Fold it into three, turn it 90° and put it through the machine again.

2 Rolling the dough. Gradually reduce the roller setting so that the dough becomes thinner and thinner. The dough should not be folded again.

3 Preparing the sauce. Cut the cheese into small pieces and place in the pan with the butter. Melt over a gentle heat, stirring all the time, then add the cream.

4 Put the spaghetti in the sauce. Put the drained noodles into the cream sauce and toss and turn them gently with two forks so that all strands are coated with the sauce.

Our tip

If you use a pasta machine, you will need someone to help with the rolling and cutting of the long noodles. If you wish to try the recipe and do not have a pasta machine, knead the dough by hand at the first stage until it is smooth and elastic. Rest the dough and then roll out small portions on a floured surface until they are very thin. Cut into thin strips, or roll up and cut into thin strips before unrolling the separate strands.

Stuffed Onions

These onions with their hearty kale or spinach stuffing go particularly well with pork dishes and roast goose or duck.

Serves 4

---

1 lb kale or spinach
salt
4 large onions (each weighing about 14 oz)
freshly ground black pepper
pinch sugar
6 tablespoons goose fat or lard
3–4 tablespoons hot beef broth
½ cup soft bread crumbs

Preparation time: 1¼ hours

Remove the kale or spinach leaves from the stalks and rinse them thoroughly in cold water. Blanch in boiling salted water for 5 minutes. Tip the kale or spinach into a colander and rinse under cold running water. Drain well, then chop as finely as possible.

Preheat the oven to 400°F. Meanwhile, fill a second saucepan with salted water and bring to a boil. Peel the onions and place in the boiling water. Cook for about 5–10 minutes or until they are just tender – the cooking time depends on the size of the onions. Drain well and allow to cool.

Cut a "lid" from the top of each onion and press out the centers with the fingertips so that only two or three outside layers remain. Chop the "lids" and centers as finely as possible. Mix the chopped onion into the spinach or kale. Season to taste with salt, pepper and sugar. Melt about 2 tablespoons of the goose fat or lard in a saucepan and add the kale or spinach mixture with the broth, then cover and cook for 5 minutes.

Grease a baking dish with a little of the remaining goose fat or lard. Stuff the onions with the kale or spinach mixture, heaping it up on top. Sprinkle with the bread crumbs and dot with the rest of the goose fat or lard. Place the onions in the dish and then in the heated oven. Bake for 15 minutes, then reduce the temperature to 300°F. Bake for 10–15 minutes longer.

Serve the onions as soon as they are ready so that none of the delicious aroma is lost.

Our tip

The amount of filling needed will depend on the size of the onions. If the onions are small, provide two per person. If any filling is left over, spread it over the bottom of the dish and make little depressions to stand each onion in. Sprinkle the leftover stuffing with bread crumbs and dot with goose fat or lard so that it does not become dry.

1 **Removing the centers of the onions.** Press out the center of each onion so that only two or three outside layers remain. Chop the centers very finely and mix with the kale or spinach.

2 **Cooking the kale or spinach.** Heat the goose fat or lard in a saucepan. Add the kale or spinach mixture and broth, then cover and cook for 5 minutes.

3 **Stuffing the onions.** Place the kale or spinach mixture in the hollowed-out onions, mounding it up on top. Sprinkle with bread crumbs and dot with goose fat or lard.

Eggplant with Tsatsiki

Eggplant with tsatsiki is a Greek specialty that has rapidly gained in popularity in Europe in recent years. It is a light summer dish that can be served as an appetizer or as a light snack.

1 eggplant about 1¾ lb
salt
1¼ cups plain yogurt
juice ½ lemon
2–3 cloves garlic
½ bunch fresh dill
½ cucumber
freshly ground white pepper
flour
6–8 tablespoons olive oil

Preparation time: 45 minutes

Rinse and dry the eggplant and trim off the ends. Cut the eggplant on a slant into slices ½ inch thick. Lay the slices next to one another on a plate and sprinkle both sides with salt. Leave for about 20 minutes to allow excess moisture and bitter juices to be drawn out.

During this time the tsatsiki can be prepared. Mix the yogurt with the lemon juice. Peel the garlic and chop as finely as possible or crush over the yogurt with a garlic press. Rinse the dill, shake dry and chop finely. Stir into the yogurt with the garlic. Wipe the cucumber and grate over the mixture. Season generously with salt and pepper, then beat vigorously until the tsatsiki is light and frothy. The process of beating will distribute and enhance the flavors of the ingredients. Cover the dish and put in the refrigerator to chill.

Rinse the eggplant slices and pat dry with paper towels. Dredge each slice with flour. This is best done by pressing both sides of each slice into the flour and shaking off the excess flour afterwards. Heat a few tablespoons of oil in a skillet and fry the eggplant, a few slices at a time, over a high heat until they are golden brown on both sides. Add more oil to the pan if necessary. Turn the slices only once to prevent them breaking. Remove from the pan and drain on paper towels. Pat the upper surfaces with paper towels as well so that all the oil is removed; eggplants tend to absorb a good deal of oil during frying.

Serve the eggplant hot or cold with the tsatsiki poured over it. Fresh French bread and well-drained ripe olives make excellent accompaniments.

1 **Salt the eggplant.** Lay the slices next to one another and sprinkle salt on both sides. Set aside for about 20 minutes to allow the bitter juices and excess moisture to be drawn out.

2 **Preparing the tsatsiki.** Grate the cucumber over the yogurt. Season to taste with salt and pepper. Beat well to distribute the flavors evenly, then cover and chill while frying the eggplant.

3 **Frying the eggplant.** Heat the oil in a skillet and fry the eggplant, a few slices at a time, until both sides are golden brown. Drain well on paper towels.

Our tip

Zucchini can be prepared in the same way and served with tsatsiki. The process of sprinkling with salt can be omitted unless the zucchini are very watery.

Lasagne Verdi al Forno

The hearts of pasta lovers everywhere beat faster at the thought of lasagne al forno. This versatile dish can be served as a main course with salad or as an appetizer. As the latter this quantity will serve 10 people.

Serves 6

4 slices bacon
1 onion
1 clove garlic
1 stalk celery
1 carrot
2 large ripe tomatoes
2 tablespoons olive oil
5 oz (about ¾ cup)
mixed ground pork and beef
6 tablespoons hot beef broth
2 tablespoons red wine
1 tablespoon tomato paste
salt
freshly ground black pepper
pinch sugar
2 sprigs fresh oregano
2 sprigs fresh parsley
5 tablespoons butter
¼ cup flour
3 cups hot milk
grated nutmeg
½ lb mozzarella cheese
butter for greasing dish
5 tablespoons cream
about ½ lb green lasagne
(see tip)
¾ cup grated Parmesan cheese

Preparation time: 2 hours

The meat sauce should be prepared first. Chop the bacon into small pieces. Peel the onion and garlic. Trim the celery and peel or scrape the carrot. Chop all the vegetables into very small dice. Scald the tomatoes in boiling water for 10 seconds, then peel and remove the core and any pieces of hard stem. Cut the tomatoes in half so that all seed chambers are visible and, taking half a tomato at a time in the palm of your hand, squeeze gently until the seeds fall out. Discard, and chop the tomatoes very finely.

Put the bacon in a large saucepan and fry until the fat runs out. Add the olive oil and then the onion, garlic, celery and carrot. Fry, stirring all the time, until the vegetables are softened and any moisture has evaporated. Add the ground meat and fry until it becomes browned and crumbly in appearance. Stir in the tomatoes, broth, red wine and tomato paste. Season to taste with salt, pepper and sugar and bring to a boil quickly.

Rinse the oregano and parsley, shake dry and chop finely. Stir the herbs into the sauce, then reduce the heat and simmer gently for 20 minutes, stirring occasionally.

While the meat sauce is cooking, prepare the cream sauce. Melt the butter in a saucepan and stir in the flour. Cook for 1 minute, then gradually add the hot milk, stirring all the time. Bring to a boil, stirring, and simmer for 10 minutes. Season with a little grated nutmeg and salt and pepper to taste.

Chop the mozzarella cheese into small pieces. Grease a rectangular baking dish with butter. Preheat the oven to 400°F. When the meat sauce is ready, stir in the cream.

To assemble the lasagne, start with a thin layer of cream sauce in the baking dish and cover with sheets of pasta. Then add a thin layer of meat sauce which should be spread out evenly. Pour another layer of cream sauce over the meat sauce, and sprinkle a little Parmesan cheese and a few pieces of mozzarella cheese over it. Place a few more sheets of pasta on top of the cheese, making sure that they do not overlap. Continue the layers, finishing with cream sauce and cheese. Place in the heated oven and bake for 25–30 minutes. Serve immediately.

Our tip

Read the instructions for cooking the pasta carefully before preparing the dish – some pasta needs to be precooked. If this is the case, rinse the sheets of pasta under cold running water after cooking and spread them out on a clean dish towel to drain thoroughly. Start with a layer of pasta when assembling the ingredients in the dish. If it is not necessary to precook the pasta, the first layer should always be of cream sauce.

1 **Seasoning the cream sauce.** Season the sauce with a little freshly grated nutmeg and salt, but a generous amount of pepper, and beat lightly and briefly to combine.

2 **Spreading the meat sauce.** Spread out a thin layer of meat sauce evenly on top of the pasta using a flat spoon or spatula. Be sure all the pasta is covered.

3 **Adding the cream sauce.** Pour a little sauce over the meat sauce and sprinkle with a little Parmesan cheese and a few pieces of mozzarella cheese.

4 **Arranging the lasagne.** Lay the sheets of lasagne next to one another on top of the layer of cheese. The final layer should be of cream sauce and cheese.

Baked Endive with Ham

Baked endive wrapped in ham is a dish for all occasions. It can be served as an appetizer during a full-scale dinner or as part of a light meal.

Serves 4

---

4 heads Belgian endive
3 tablespoons butter
6 tablespoons hot chicken broth
juice ½ lemon
salt
freshly ground white pepper
grated nutmeg
¾ cup heavy cream
4 thin slices cooked ham
1 cup grated Gruyère or
Swiss cheese

Preparation time: 45 minutes

Remove any of the outer leaves from the endive that are brown or wilted. Rinse and pat dry. Take each head and cut a small cone-shaped piece from the base, without damaging the outer leaves. This part of the vegetable contains the bitter substances that sometimes give it an overwhelming flavor.

Preheat the oven to 425°F. Grease an oval baking dish with 1 tablespoon of the butter. Place the rest of the butter in a skillet and add the endive. Cook gently over a moderate heat, turning occasionally. As soon as the outer leaves become a little transparent – they should not change color – add the hot chicken broth and lemon juice. Season to taste with salt, pepper and nutmeg. Bring to a boil, then stir in the cream, being careful not to damage the endive. Cover the pan and cook gently for a further 5–6 minutes.

Place a slice of ham on a round skimming spoon. Remove a head of endive from the pan with a fork. Allow the excess sauce to drip off, then place the endive on the ham and roll it up. Hold the skimming spoon over the pan during this process so that any sauce from the endive drips back into the pan. Place each endive and ham roll in the baking dish.

Turn up the heat under the skillet and boil the sauce until it has reduced to about half the quantity. Season again with salt, pepper and nutmeg. Stir half of the cheese into the sauce until melted and smooth. Pour the sauce over the endive and ham rolls, shaking the dish to distribute the sauce evenly. Sprinkle the remaining cheese over the top so that the surface is well covered. Place the dish in the heated oven and bake for 15 minutes. Serve immediately or the cheese will lose a lot of its flavor.

New potatoes with chopped parsley or mashed potatoes with herbs go well with this dish.

1 **Removing the bitter core.** Cut a small cone-shaped piece out of the base of each head of endive without damaging the outer leaves. This part of the vegetable is quite bitter.

2 **Wrapping the endive.** Remove each head of endive from the pan with a fork, allow excess sauce to drain off, then lay the endive on the ham and roll it up.

3 **Sprinkling with cheese.** If the cheese is distributed evenly over the endive and ham rolls, it will brown evenly and develop its full aroma. Bake until melted and golden.

Our tip

It is possible to make this dish with other vegetables, for example salsify or leeks. If the vegetables used are thin, wrap more than one piece in each slice of ham. The recipe is particularly good made with asparagus or canned heart palms. Many kinds of ham can also be used; try prosciutto, or ham cooked in wine or flavored with herbs.

Cheese Soufflé

A good soufflé can be produced even by a beginning cook. Simply follow the instructions, make sure there are no drafts in the kitchen and serve the soufflé straight from the oven.

---

butter for greasing dish
1 cup grated Gruyère or
Swiss cheese
5 tablespoons butter
5 tablespoons flour
1¼ cups hot milk
salt
freshly ground white pepper
grated nutmeg
4 eggs

Preparation time: 1 hour

Butter a soufflé dish (about 8 inches in diameter). Sprinkle a little of the cheese over the inside of the dish. Preheat the oven to 400°F. To make the roux, melt the butter in a saucepan and stir in the flour. Cook, stirring, for 1–2 minutes or until the mixture has become creamy in color and a little frothy. It should not become brown. Gradually stir in the hot milk and continue stirring until it is well blended. Bring to a boil and simmer, stirring, until the sauce becomes thick and creamy. Season to taste with salt, pepper and nutmeg. Remove from the heat and allow to cool slightly.

Separate the eggs. Add the egg yolks to the sauce, one at a time. It is important that each yolk is beaten into the sauce thoroughly before the next is added so that the mixture is perfectly smooth. When all the yolks have been beaten in, pour the mixture into a large bowl.

Put 1 teaspoon of the remaining cheese aside for later use and stir the rest into the mixture until melted and smooth. Beat the egg whites in a separate bowl until stiff peaks form. Tip the egg white onto the cheese mixture and fold in gently but quickly, using a metal spoon. Do not stir or the air beaten into the egg whites will be lost.

Spoon the mixture without delay into the soufflé dish; it should come about halfway up the sides of the dish, leaving enough room to rise. Sprinkle the reserved cheese over the top and place in the heated oven. Bake for 25–30 minutes or until the surface is golden brown and the soufflé has risen above the rim of the dish. The soufflé should be a little creamy in the center – on no account dry and hard. Remove from the oven and serve immediately.

1 **Making the roux.** Stirring all the time, blend the butter and flour together over a moderate heat until the paste is creamy in color and a little frothy.

2 **Adding the milk.** Pour in the hot milk, a little at a time, and stir until the ingredients are well blended. Continue to stir until the sauce becomes thick.

3 **Add the egg yolks singly.** It is important that each yolk is beaten separately into the mixture, so that it can be completely absorbed. Stir in the cheese.

4 **Folding in the egg whites.** Fold the egg whites into the mixture gently but quickly so that the mixture remains light and airy. Spoon the mixture into the dish.

Peanut Broccoli Flan

This delicious peanut pastry case with its broccoli, ham and cream filling, covered with crisp toasted cheese, makes an excellent light meal accompanied by a fresh white wine or beer.

Serves 8

1 cup roasted salted peanuts
2 cups flour
salt
$\frac{1}{8}$ teaspoon cayenne pepper
7 eggs
2 tablespoons ice water
6 tablespoons cold butter
2 lb fresh broccoli or $1\frac{1}{4}$ lb frozen broccoli
$\frac{1}{2}$ lb cooked ham
small bunch fresh parsley
2 cups light cream
$\frac{3}{4}$ cup grated Gruyère or Swiss cheese
freshly ground white pepper
grated nutmeg

Cooling time: 1 hour
Preparation time: $1\frac{1}{2}$ hours

Place the peanuts in a plastic bag and crush them with a rolling pin or a heavy bottle until they are almost ground to a paste, or grind in a food processor. Sift the flour onto a work surface and add the crushed peanuts, a pinch of salt and the cayenne pepper. Make a hollow in the center. Break one of the eggs into the depression and add the ice water. Cut the butter into small pieces and place around the edges of the flour.

Knead the ingredients together to form a smooth dough, using your fingertips. Knead as quickly as possible so that the ingredients, particularly the butter, do not become warm. If they do, the resulting pastry may be heavy. Shape the dough into a ball, wrap in foil and place in the refrigerator to rest for 1 hour.

Meanwhile, prepare the filling. If fresh broccoli is to be used, remove any wilted leaves or hard stalks. Rinse and drain, then separate the tiny florets. Chop the tender stalks into short pieces. Cook the broccoli florets and stalks in boiling salted water for 8–10 minutes. Frozen broccoli can be placed unthawed in boiling salted water and cooked for 4 minutes. Drain and rinse under cold running water. Drain again and put aside to cool.

Preheat the oven to 400°F. Remove any fat from the ham and cut it into strips. Rinse the parsley, shake it dry and chop finely. Beat the remaining eggs together and stir in the cream. Stir half of the cheese into the egg mixture. Season generously with salt and pepper and a little grated nutmeg.

Roll out the dough on a floured surface and use to line a 9 inch springform cake pan or other deep cake pan. Place the broccoli, ham and parsley in the pastry case. Pour the egg and cheese mixture evenly over the ingredients and sprinkle the rest of the grated cheese over the top.

Place immediately in the heated oven so that the pastry cannot become soft and soggy. Bake for 25 minutes, then reduce the temperature to 225°F and bake for a further 25 minutes. After removing from the oven, let the quiche stand for 10 minutes before cutting it into equal portions.

Our tip

The pastry case is particularly delicious when made with wholewheat flour. Try other fillings, too, for example spinach or a mixture of vegetables (such as peas, diced carrots and small pieces of cauliflower) with small pieces of fried bacon instead of ham. Take the saltiness of the bacon into account and reduce the seasoning accordingly. There is no limit to the interesting fillings an imaginative cook can invent.

1 **Crushing the peanuts.** Place the nuts in a plastic bag and crush them with a rolling pin or heavy bottle until almost ground to a paste, or use a processor for grinding.

2 **Lining the pan.** Roll out the dough and use to line the pan. This can be done by cutting a round for the base and a strip for the side. Cut a thin strip to seal the join.

3 **Filling the quiche.** Place the broccoli, ham and parsley in the pastry case. Pour the egg mixture evenly over the ingredients and then sprinkle with the rest of the cheese.

Blinis with Caviar

Blinis can be served with caviar, sour cream and fresh butter as a main dish for four or as an appetizer or snack for eight. They are delicious on any occasion.

Serves 4

1¼ cups all-purpose flour
1 cake (0.6 oz) compressed yeast
pinch sugar
¼ cup lukewarm water
8 eggs
⅛ teaspoon salt
½ cup buckwheat flour
(available in health food stores)
2 cups lukewarm milk
¾ cup light cream
2 cups sour cream
1 cup (½ lb) butter
½ lb caviar

Resting time: 30 minutes
Preparation time: 45 minutes

Making sure the all-purpose flour is at room temperature, sift it into a bowl. Make a hollow in the middle, crumble the yeast into it and sprinkle with the sugar. Pour the lukewarm water over the yeast and sugar and cream them together. Mix in a little flour to make a batter. Cover the bowl and leave in a warm place for 15 minutes. Meanwhile, separate the eggs. Beat the egg yolks with the salt until creamy.

When the batter has doubled in size and acquired a honeycombed appearance, add the buckwheat flour and beaten egg yolks. Stir all the flour and the egg yolks into the batter, then gradually add the warm milk. Cover the bowl again with a cloth and leave to rise in a warm place for 10–15 minutes.

Stir the light cream and ¾ cup of the sour cream into the batter. Beat the egg whites until stiff peaks form and fold gently into the batter with a balloon whisk until everything is well blended. Do not beat.

Melt a little of the butter in a skillet. Using a tablespoon, drop the batter into the pan to form pancakes about 3 inches in diameter. Cook until bubbles appear on the surface and the undersides are golden, then turn and lightly brown the other sides. Drain the blinis on paper towels, then place in a clean dish towel. Keep them warm in the oven turned to its lowest setting until all are ready.

Form the remaining butter into curls, or melt it. Place the remaining sour cream in a small serving dish. Serve the caviar in a bowl on a bed of ice cubes or in a decorative dish. Stack the blinis on a heated serving plate and serve immediately with the caviar, sour cream and butter.

1 **Creaming the yeast.** Add the water to the yeast and sugar and cream them together. Mix in a little flour to make a pool of batter. Leave in a warm place for 15 minutes.

2 **Preparing the batter.** Add the buckwheat flour and the beaten egg yolks to the mixture in the bowl and stir in the lukewarm milk gradually until smooth.

3 **Folding in the egg whites.** Beat the egg whites to stiff peaks and fold carefully into the batter with a balloon whisk so that they combine well. Do not beat.

4 **Frying the blinis.** Melt some butter in a skillet. Place the batter in the pan with a tablespoon to form pancakes about 3 inches in diameter and cook until golden.

Our tip

Smoked sturgeon or smoked salmon are often served instead of caviar with blinis in Russia. We have used salmon roe which is not as expensive as the genuine thing, but for general purposes it is a reasonable substitute and is easier on the pocket.

Sherried Eggs with Snow Peas

Sherried eggs look like fried eggs but are in fact cooked in spicy chicken broth. They taste particularly good with tender snow peas cooked in butter.

Serves 4

1¾ lb snow peas
salt
3 tablespoons butter
½ teaspoon lemon juice
freshly ground white pepper
grated nutmeg
6 tablespoons chicken broth
6 tablespoons dry sherry
¼ teaspoon Worcestershire sauce
4 fresh eggs
handful fresh chervil leaves

Preparation time: 30 minutes

Prepare the peas by cutting off the stalks, pulling off any threads at the same time. Remove the tips of the pods, pulling off any threads on the other side as well. Rinse the prepared peas quickly in cold water and drain. Bring a large pan of salted water to a boil. Fill a large bowl with cold water and ice cubes.

The peas must now be blanched so that they retain their fresh green color. This is done by placing them, a handful at a time, in the fiercely boiling water for 2 minutes, then removing them and plunging them into the ice cold water in the bowl. Remove them after a few seconds and place in a colander or sieve to drain.

Melt 2 tablespoons of the butter in a saucepan and add the drained peas. Season to taste with the lemon juice, salt, pepper and a little grated nutmeg. Cover the pan and warm the peas through over a gentle heat. Shake the pan frequently so that they do not stick.

Meanwhile, heat the chicken broth in a skillet with the remaining butter, the sherry and Worcestershire sauce. As soon as the mixture begins to boil, break two eggs into it. Simmer for 4–5 minutes or until the egg whites are set. Remove them from the pan and keep hot while you cook the remaining eggs in the same way. The sherry mixture should be boiling fiercely when the eggs are placed in the pan; however, the heat can be turned down once they are in so that the liquid does not evaporate. This would make the eggs hard and rubbery.

While the eggs are cooking, rinse the chervil under cold, running water, shake dry and chop.

Place the eggs on heated plates. Season the egg whites with a little salt and pepper and sprinkle a few drops of the hot sherry mixture over them. Season the peas and place next to the eggs on the plates. Sprinkle with chopped chervil and serve immediately. New potatoes with butter or sautéed potatoes go well with this dish.

1 **Preparing the peas.** Cut the stalk ends off the pea pods, pulling off any threads at the same time. Cut off the tips of the pods and remove any threads on the other side as well.

2 **Blanching the peas.** Cook the peas for 2 minutes in fiercely boiling salted water, then plunge into ice cold water. They will retain their color if cooked this way. Drain well.

3 **Cooking the eggs.** As soon as the sherry mixture is boiling, break two eggs into the liquid. Cook for 4–5 minutes or until the whites are set, then remove the eggs from the pan. Cook the remaining two eggs the same way.

Our tip

You can compose dishes of your own using this recipe as a basis. Try cooking the eggs in seasoned chicken broth flavored with white port or Madeira. You can use other vegetables as well, for example, blanched asparagus tips or tender young green beans cooked in butter. Lettuce strips, mushrooms or peeled, seeded tomatoes and herbs cooked in butter make wonderful alternatives. Whichever vegetable you use, do not overcook it. It should retain the "bite" and freshness of the raw vegetable.

Poached Eggs in Dill and Mustard Sauce

Poached eggs in dill and mustard sauce turns a simple ingredient into a special supper dish. Serve with boiled potatoes and green salad or with toast points.

Serves 4

---

about 1 gallon water
¼ cup white wine vinegar
1 shallot
1 bunch fresh dill
2 sprigs fresh parsley
¼ lemon
8 fresh eggs
2 tablespoons butter
1 teaspoon flour
1–2 tablespoons prepared mustard
6 tablespoons dry white wine
1 cup heavy cream
salt
freshly ground white pepper
pinch sugar
Worcestershire sauce

Preparation time: 30–45 minutes

Even the most experienced cooks find poaching eggs to be a tricky business. It is made easier when really fresh eggs are used; eggs that are more than 5 or 6 days old are no longer suitable for poaching. It is also important to have the ingredients prepared and ready before cooking the eggs to prevent them becoming dry or cold.

Place the water in a large saucepan so that it comes 2–3 inches up the sides. Add the vinegar and bring to a boil. It is necessary to have a large amount of water so that it does not cease boiling when the eggs are put in; this will prevent them sticking to the bottom.

While the water is coming to a boil, prepare the ingredients. Peel and finely chop the shallot. Rinse the herbs, shake them dry and chop very finely. Rinse and dry the lemon and grate the rind.

As soon as the water is boiling, switch off the heat, but leave the saucepan on the range. Break one of the eggs into a cup. Take a ladle, dip it in the boiling water for a few seconds, then remove and slide the egg into it. Place the ladle on the surface of the water, then roll the egg over into

the water so that the egg white closes around the yolk and the egg acquires a neat oval shape.

Repeat with three more eggs, then cover the pan and cook for about 3 minutes. Remove the eggs with a slotted spoon and place each for a second in cold water so that it does not continue to cook on the inside. Poached eggs are ready when the white is firm but the yolk still soft. To test if an egg is ready, remove from the water on the slotted spoon and press the egg yolk gently. If the eggs are overcooked, the yolks will be hard and rubbery. This can easily happen if the heat under the pan is too strong.

When the first four eggs have been cooked and are draining, bring the water to a boil again. Turn off the heat and poach the remaining eggs in the same fashion. When all the eggs are ready, take a sharp knife and trim off any loose or untidy pieces of egg white so that the eggs are neat and oval in appearance.

To make the sauce, melt the butter in a saucepan and fry the shallot until it is soft. Stir in the flour and cook for a few minutes, stirring all the time, until it begins to bubble. Stir in the mustard, then gradually add the wine and cream, stirring continually. Increase the heat and cook the sauce, stirring all the time, until it becomes thick and creamy. Season to taste with salt, pepper, sugar and Worcestershire sauce and stir in the grated lemon rind, parsley and dill.

Place the eggs in the sauce and cook very gently for 5 minutes. Baste the eggs frequently with the sauce so that they acquire some of its fragrance. The sauce must on no account simmer but just be kept warm over a very gentle heat. Serve hot.

If it is too difficult to poach more than two eggs at a time, warm them through again in hot salted water before placing them in the sauce. Eggs which have been poached and then placed for a moment in cold water will not start to cook through again. Another trick which helps make nicely shaped eggs is to make a whirlpool in the boiling water by stirring with a spoon and to slide the egg directly into the center of the whirlpool.

1 **Sliding an egg into the ladle.** Break one egg into a cup. Dip the ladle in the saucepan of boiling water for a moment before sliding the egg into the ladle.

2 **Poaching the egg.** Place the ladle on the surface of the water, then roll the egg over into the water so that the egg white closes around the yolk.

3 **Trimming the eggs.** Cut off any loose or untidy pieces of egg white with a sharp knife so that the egg acquires a neat oval shape.

4 **Place the eggs in the sauce** and heat for 5 minutes, basting them frequently. Keep the sauce warm over a very gentle heat, and do not allow to simmer.

Deep-fried Eggs on Green Asparagus

Eggs deep fried in oil – what the French call "oeufs frits" – puff up like fritters and create an interesting contrast for the palate between the crisp egg white on the outside and the soft yolk inside. They are particularly delicious served on a bed of asparagus pieces.

Serves 4

1¾ lb fresh asparagus
salt
3 tablespoons butter
freshly ground white pepper
lemon juice
about 1 cup vegetable oil
4 very fresh eggs

Preparation time: 30 minutes

Rinse the asparagus carefully in cold water, paying particular attention to the tips as there may still be a little sand or dirt hidden in them. Drain. Trim the bases, cutting off any woody stems. Scrape each asparagus stem carefully with a sharp knife, working from the tip towards the base. Lay two or three asparagus spears next to one another on a board and cut on a slant into ¾ inch lengths.

Bring plenty of salted water to a boil in a large saucepan and cook the asparagus for 1 minute. Place in a colander to drain. Heat the butter in a skillet until it starts to bubble. Add the asparagus and cook, shaking the pan vigorously to prevent it from sticking, until just tender. Season to taste with salt, pepper and lemon juice. Keep warm until the eggs are ready.

Pour the oil into a small, deep skillet – the oil should be about ¾ inch deep – and heat it. Test the heat by putting a small cube of bread into the oil; when it turns brown immediately, the oil is at the correct temperature. Now tilt the pan slightly and slide in an egg. It is advisable to wear oven gloves during this process as the fat tends to spit. As soon as the egg is in the pan, fold the white over the yolk with a spoon so that the yolk is completely enveloped and cannot become hard or stick to the pan. Baste the egg with oil frequently so that the white

becomes crisp and brown. Remove from the pan with a slotted spoon and place on a thick layer of paper towels to drain. Fry the remaining eggs quickly in the same manner.

Make a bed of asparagus on four heated plates and place an egg in the middle of each one. Season with a little salt and pepper and serve immediately.

Our tip

Fresh eggs are essential for success with this recipe. If you are not sure if the eggs are fresh, test one by breaking it onto a plate. If the egg is fresh, the yolk will be round and the white thick and viscous. If the egg yolk is flat and the white thin and watery, the egg is not fresh. It is possible to test an egg for freshness without cracking it. Slide the egg into a glass of water. A fresh egg will sink to the bottom and lie on its side; an older egg will half float in the water with one end pointing to the surface – this is because it has become lighter due to loss of moisture.

1 **Sauté the asparagus.** Heat the butter in a skillet until it begins to bubble. Add the asparagus and sauté quickly until just tender, shaking the pan to prevent sticking.

2 **Folding over the egg white.** As soon as the egg is in the pan of oil, fold the white over the yolk with a spoon so that the yolk is completely enveloped.

3 **Frying the egg.** Baste the egg frequently with the hot oil so that the white becomes crisp and brown. Remove with a slotted spoon and drain on paper towels.

Fish Twists with Shrimp

Fish twists with shrimp look like small works of art. The secret lies in buying really fresh fish; the twists form by themselves during the cooking process.

Serves 4

2 lb sole or flounder
1 cup water
1 cup dry white wine
1 onion
3 sprigs fresh parsley
1 leek
1 stalk celery
1 carrot
salt
freshly ground white pepper
juice $\frac{1}{4}$ lemon
$\frac{1}{2}$ lb small shelled cooked shrimp
1–2 tablespoons dry vermouth
2 egg yolks
3 tablespoons butter
2 sprigs fresh dill

Preparation time: 1 hour

If you buy the fish already filleted, ask the fish merchant for extra bones and trimmings. Rinse the bones and trimmings in cold water, place in a medium-sized saucepan and add the water and wine. The liquid should cover the bones and trimmings. Peel the onion. Rinse the parsley and shake dry. Trim the leek and celery. Peel the carrot. Chop the vegetables and parsley coarsely and place in the saucepan. Bring to a boil, then reduce to a simmer and cook gently for 15 minutes, occasionally skimming off any scum which forms on the surface.

Meanwhile, rinse the fish fillets under cold running water and pat dry. Lay the fillets on a wooden board and cut them in half lengthwise, following the grain of the flesh which narrows at the tail. Season to taste on both sides with salt, pepper and lemon juice.

Strain the stock through a fine sieve or paper coffee filter and return to the saucepan. Bring to a boil again. Reduce the heat and place the shrimp in the stock. Cook for 1–2 minutes to warm through. Remove with a slotted spoon, place on a large plate with a little of the hot stock and keep warm.

Heat the stock again until it is boiling fiercely, then remove from the heat (do not switch off the heat). Place a few fillet strips in the stock. The fillets will cook through in about 1 minute during which time they will draw together into twists. Remove with a slotted spoon, place on a spoon and put on the plate with the shrimp. Bring the stock to a boil again and repeat the process until all the fillet strips are cooked. Keep hot.

Bring the stock to a boil again over a fierce heat and boil rapidly in the open pan for 10 minutes or until the liquid has reduced to about 1 cup. Season to taste with salt, pepper and the dry vermouth and remove the pan from the heat. Cool slightly, then mix 1 tablespoon of the stock with the beaten egg yolks. Strain the mixture through a sieve into the remaining stock, beating vigorously with a balloon whisk. Heat the sauce once again, whisking constantly, but do not allow it to boil. When it has thickened, remove from the heat. Chop the butter into small pieces and beat it into the sauce, a piece at a time.

Rinse the dill, shake it dry and chop coarsely. Drain any excess stock from the fish twists and shrimp, then place on a heated serving plate. Pour the hot sauce over the fish, garnish with dill and serve immediately.

1 **Dividing the fillets.** Place the fillets on a wooden board and divide each in half lengthwise, following the grain of the flesh. Season with salt, pepper and lemon juice.

2 **Cooking the fish twists.** Place a few fillets in the hot stock and cook for 1 minute; they will draw together into twists during this brief cooking. Drain and keep hot.

3 **Thickening the sauce.** Mix a little stock with the egg yolks, then strain the mixture through a sieve into the stock which should be hot but not boiling. Beat vigorously with a balloon whisk.

Our tip

Fish twists can be made from any kind of white fish as long as it is really fresh. Frozen fish is not suitable for this dish as the fish flesh no longer possesses enough tension to draw into twists while cooking.

Seafood in Butter Sauce

This exquisite dish requires spoons as well as knives and forks so that the delicate butter sauce can be enjoyed to the last drop.

Serves 4

---

4 jumbo shrimp
8 sea scallops
8 fresh oysters
½ lb white fish fillets
1–2 boiled crabs or a small boiled lobster
2 shallots
6 tablespoons water
1 cup dry white wine
freshly ground white pepper
1 cup (½ lb) butter
small pinch salt
little dry vermouth or dry sherry
1 sprig fresh dill

Preparation time: 1½–2 hours

Clean the shrimp. Cut in half lengthwise and remove the black vein-like intestine that runs along the back. Rinse and pat dry. Pat the scallops dry with paper towels. Chop each into two or three pieces.

If the oysters are still in their shells, open them as follows: lay the oysters on a folded dish towel with the flat side of the shell facing upwards. Grip each oyster firmly between the fold of the towel with one hand and open it with an oyster knife. This is done by firmly pressing the knife into the hinge of the shell and ramming it in horizontally. Force the two shell halves apart, running the flat side of the knife around the edges of the upper shell. Lift off the upper shell and remove the oyster from the bottom half, separating the muscle as you do so.

Cut the white fish fillet into bite-sized pieces. Remove the white crabmeat, or lobster meat, from the shells. Chop lobster meat into bite-sized pieces.

Peel the shallots and chop very finely. Place in a small saucepan with the water, wine and a little pepper. Bring to a boil and simmer for 5–10 minutes or until the shallot is soft. Remove the pan from the heat and cook the seafood gently in the hot stock in the following order: first the shrimp and white fish fillet, then the scallops, and then the oysters. If necessary, keep placing the pan on the heat again and bringing the stock to simmering point so that it is hot enough to cook the fish and shellfish in the short time. As a guide to cooking times: the shrimp will need 2–3 minutes' cooking time, the white fish fillet 2–3 minutes, the scallops 1–2 minutes and the oysters 1 minute. When everything is ready, remove from the stock with a slotted spoon, put on a warm plate and sprinkle with a little hot stock. Cover and keep warm until the sauce is made.

Boil down the stock over a fierce heat until reduced to about 6 tablespoons. Meanwhile, cut the butter into pieces. Beat one-quarter of the butter into the stock. As soon as the liquid begins to bubble, remove the pan from the heat and beat in the rest of the butter a piece at a time. The sauce will gradually become white, creamy in texture and frothy.

Season to taste with a very little salt and a little dry vermouth or sherry. Place the seafood in the sauce, garnish with the dill and serve immediately.

Our tip

The pieces of shallot can remain in the butter sauce if they are very finely chopped. If they are too big, strain the stock before or after reducing the liquid. Another way to make the butter sauce is to put the reduced stock into the blender jar and to add the butter a piece at a time while processing. This must be done very quickly so that the sauce does not become cold.

1 **Halving the shrimp.** Cut the shrimp in half lengthwise and remove the intestine which runs along the back like a black vein. Rinse and pat dry.

2 **Preparing the scallops.** Dry the scallops by patting them with paper towels. Cut the white flesh into two or three pieces.

3 **Opening the oysters.** Press the tip of the knife into the hinge of the oyster shell and ram into the oyster horizontally. Force the shells apart and remove the oyster.

4 **Beating in the butter.** As soon as the liquid becomes frothy, remove the pan from the heat and whisk in the rest of the chopped butter until the sauce is creamy.

Paupiettes of Sole Stuffed with Shrimp

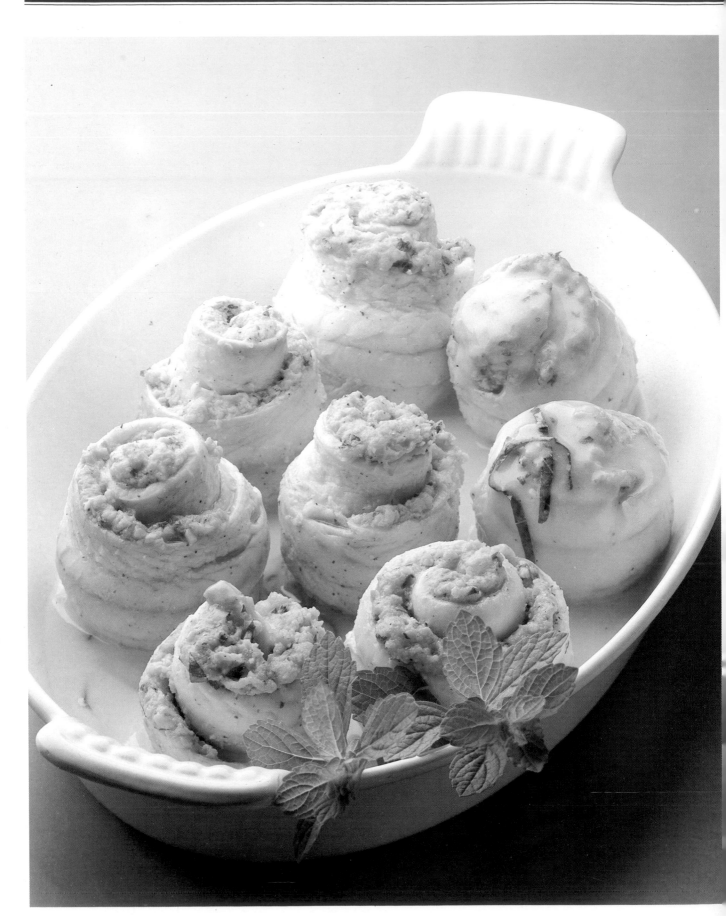

Paupiettes of sole stuffed with shrimp and mushrooms and served in a delicate creamy sauce make an excellent fish course for a special dinner.

Serves 4

8 sole fillets, each
weighing 2 oz
salt
freshly ground white pepper
juice ½ lemon
1 cup button mushrooms
1 shallot
5 tablespoons butter
½ lb cooked shelled shrimp
1 egg yolk
¾ cup heavy cream
small bunch fresh lemon balm or
juice and grated rind of ½ lemon
butter for greasing dish
1 cup dry white wine

Preparation time: 1 hour

Preheat the oven to 400°F. Pat the fillets dry with paper towels and season on both sides with a little salt, pepper and lemon juice.

Clean the mushrooms. Chop very finely and sprinkle with the rest of the lemon juice. Peel the shallot and chop very finely. Heat 1 tablespoon of the butter in a skillet and fry the mushrooms and shallot gently until they are soft. Remove from the pan and place in a bowl.

Chop the shrimp very finely or process to a purée. Stir into the mushroom mixture together with the egg yolk and a few drops of the cream. Season to taste with salt and pepper. Rinse the lemon balm and shake dry. Put half the lemon balm aside, and chop the rest finely. Mix with the other ingredients in the bowl.

Dry the fillets again and place them, skin side upwards, on a working surface. Divide the filling evenly among the fillets and spread it evenly over them with a knife. Roll them up towards the tail.

Butter a casserole generously and arrange the fish rolls in it as closely as possible to prevent them unrolling. If the casserole is too large, tie the fillets with thread and remove it later before serving. Dot the fillets with 2 tablespoons of the remaining butter. Pour the wine into the casserole from the side. Cover the dish with buttered parchment paper. Place in the heated oven and bake for 12–18 minutes or until the fish will flake easily when tested with a skewer.

Drain off the cooking liquid into a saucepan. Keep the fish rolls hot. Stir the cream into the liquid and boil down over a high heat, stirring all the time, until the sauce is creamy in consistency. Season to taste with salt and pepper. Remove the pan from the heat. Chop the remaining butter into small pieces and beat it into the sauce, a piece at a time, with a balloon whisk. Cut three-quarters of the remaining lemon balm into strips and stir into the sauce. Leave the sauce to rest for 2 minutes so that the flavor of the herb is absorbed.

Place the fish rolls in a heated serving dish. Pour the sauce over and around the fish and serve immediately, garnished with the rest of the lemon balm leaves.

1 **Rolling up the fillets.** Spread the filling evenly over the fillets with a knife. Roll up the fillets, working towards the tail. Place in a casserole.

2 **Placing the paupiettes in the casserole.** Place the fish rolls as close to one another as possible so that they cannot unroll. Tie them with thread if necessary.

3 **Beating in the butter.** Remove the pan from the heat and beat in the remaining butter, a piece at a time, with a balloon whisk. Stir in the lemon balm strips or grated lemon rind and juice.

Pike Quenelles in Cream and Basil Sauce

Pike quenelles in cream and basil sauce belong without doubt to the realms of haute cuisine. However, with patience and the very best ingredients, it is possible to master this recipe in your own kitchen.

---

1 pike, weighing about
2½ lb, dressed, or
other good firm fish such as
salmon, porgy, whiting or monkfish
salt
cayenne pepper
freshly ground white pepper
5 egg whites and 1 egg yolk
3 cups heavy cream
¾ lb fish bones
and trimmings (preferably from
flounder or other white fish)
2 cups water
3 cups dry white wine
1 onion
2 sprigs fresh parsley
1 small leek
1 stalk celery
1 bay leaf
4 white peppercorns
1 tablespoon dry vermouth
1 bunch fresh basil

Chilling time: 1¾–2 hours
Preparation time: 1¾ hours

Ask the fish merchant to prepare and fillet the fish, but to give you the bones and trimmings. If any very small bones remain, remove them carefully before preparing the dish. The remaining flesh should weigh about 1¼ pounds. Rinse the fish flesh under cold running water and dry thoroughly. Grind it twice, as finely as possible, or reduce to a purée in a blender or food processor. Season generously with salt, a little cayenne pepper and white pepper.

Beat the egg whites to stiff peaks and stir into the fish purée until it has been absorbed. The mixture should not be frothy, but a homogenous mass. Press the mixture through a fine sieve into a glass or metal bowl. Smooth over the surface and cover with a sheet of plastic wrap, pressing it onto the mixture lightly with the fingertips. Chill in the refrigerator for 1 hour.

Remove the plastic wrap and place the dish on a bed of ice cubes or in iced water in a larger bowl. Add 5 tablespoons of the cream to the fish mixture and stir until it has been absorbed. Repeat twice. When 15 tablespoons of the cream have been worked in, the mixture should be soft and creamy in texture. Place the bowl in the refrigerator again and chill for 15 minutes. The intensity of the seasoning will be lessened during the cooking process, so season the mixture generously. Return to the refrigerator.

Put 1 cup of the remaining cream aside and whip the rest until it is slightly stiff. Divide into three portions. Fold each portion into the fish mixture separately. Place in the refrigerator again, and leave to chill while preparing the stock.

Rinse all the fish bones and trimmings and place in a saucepan with the water and wine. Bring to a boil slowly, skimming off any scum as it rises. Peel the onion. Rinse the parsley. Trim the leek and celery. Add all these to the stock together with the bay leaf and peppercorns. Cover and simmer gently for 20 minutes. Strain the stock. Put 1 cup aside for the sauce and pour the rest into a wide saucepan. Bring back to a boil.

Remove the fish mixture from the refrigerator. To shape the quenelles, mold a little of the mixture between two tablespoons. Place a few quenelles at a time in the barely simmering stock and poach for 5–6 minutes. Put a little of the hot stock into another pan. As the quenelles are cooked, transfer them to the second pan with a slotted spoon, cover and keep warm. Before adding each batch of quenelles to be poached, bring the stock back to simmering point.

Place the stock reserved for the sauce and the remaining cream in a wide saucepan and bring to a boil. Season to taste with salt, pepper, cayenne pepper and dry vermouth. Remove the pan from the heat and allow the sauce to cool a little. Beat the egg yolk with a little of the sauce, then whisk into the remaining sauce in the pan. Heat gently, stirring, but on no account allow to boil.

Rinse the basil under cold running water, shake dry and chop roughly. Stir into the sauce and let steep for 1 minute, then add the drained quenelles and serve hot.

1 **Grinding the fish flesh.** Put the flesh twice through the finest grinding blade, or reduce it to a purée in portions in a blender or food processor.

2 **Passing the mixture through a sieve.** Press the mixture through a very fine sieve into a glass or metal bowl. Smooth over the surface of the mixture and cover.

3 **Adding the cream.** Pour in 5 tablespoons of the cream and stir until it has been thoroughly abosrobed. Repeat twice, with 5 tablespoons of cream each time, then chill.

4 **Cooking the quenelles.** Take a portion of the fish mixture and mold between two tablespoons. Place them one at a time in the simmering stock and let them cook for 5–6 minutes. Then lift them out and keep them warm.

Our tip

To produce light and airy pike quenelles, the mixture must be carefully made. Add the beaten egg whites and cream in small quantities and stir until the mixture becomes a uniform mass. Never beat the mixture, and keep to the times given in the recipe for chilling and resting the mixture.

Tuna Fish Provençale

When vegetables, delicate herbs, garlic, olive oil and wine are cooked slowly with tuna fish, the result is an incomparable harmony of flavors.

Serves 4

1 large piece of tuna
from the tail, weighing
2–2½ lb, or the same weight in
smaller tuna steaks
3–4 cloves garlic
8–10 anchovy fillets, canned
in brine
salt
freshly ground black pepper
juice ½ lemon
2 green peppers
1 lb large, ripe
but firm tomatoes
2 small zucchini
2 onions
1 bunch fresh or
2 teaspoons dried parsley
2 sprigs fresh or
½ teaspoon dried thyme
2 sprigs fresh or
½ teaspoon dried oregano
1 sprig fresh or
¼ teaspoon dried savory (optional)
16–20 ripe olives
5–6 tablespoons olive oil
1 small bay leaf
6 tablespoons full-bodied
dry white wine

Preparation time: 2 hours

Preheat the oven to 425°F. Rinse the fish and pat dry. Peel two or three of the cloves of garlic and cut lengthwise into tiny slivers. Rinse the anchovies, pat dry and chop each one into two or three pieces. Using the tip of a very sharp pointed knife, push the garlic slivers and anchovy pieces into the fish between the concentric rings of fibrous tissue (not directly into the fish flesh). Arrange the garlic and anchovy evenly over the fish, on both sides. Season very lightly with salt (the anchovies are salty) and more generously with pepper, and sprinkle with lemon juice.

Prepare the peppers by halving them lengthwise and removing the core and seeds. Rinse them under cold running water, then cut into strips. Scald the tomatoes in boiling water for 10 seconds, then peel and remove the core and any pieces of hard stem. Cut the tomatoes in half so that all seed chambers are visible and, taking half a tomato at a time in the palm of your hand, squeeze gently until the seeds fall out. Discard the seeds and cut the tomatoes into strips. Rinse the zucchini and trim off both ends. Quarter lengthwise, then cut into 1½ inch pieces.

Peel and halve the onions and cut into strips. Rinse the herbs and shake dry. Chop the parsley; strip the leaves of thyme, oregano and savory from the stalks and chop the savory leaves. Peel and chop the remaining garlic clove. Halve the olives and remove the pits.

Pour 2 tablespoons of the olive oil into a large baking dish. Arrange one-third of the onion, garlic and herbs on the bottom and sprinkle them with lemon juice. Place the tuna on the bed of vegetables. Arrange the peppers, tomatoes, zucchini and remaining herbs around and on top of the fish. Add the halved olives. Place the rest of the onion and garlic on top of the fish and sprinkle with salt and pepper. Crumble the bay leaf and sprinkle on top. Pour the rest of the olive oil over and around the fish. Pour the wine in from the side and shake the dish a little so that it is well distributed. Cover the dish and cook in the heated oven for 1½ hours, basting occasionally with the liquid.

1 **Inserting the garlic and anchovies.** Push the garlic slivers and pieces of anchovy between the concentric rings of tissue (not directly into the fish flesh) with the tip of a sharp knife.

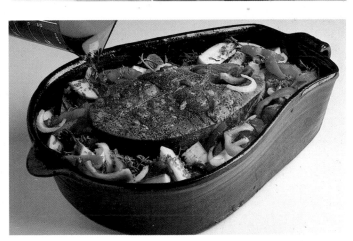

2 **Preparing the peppers.** Halve the peppers lengthwise. Pull out the core and seeds with a quick twist, then rinse under cold running water to remove any remaining seeds.

3 **Adding the liquid.** Pour the rest of the olive oil over the fish and vegetables. Pour in the wine from the side of the dish and shake the dish to distribute the liquid evenly.

Mussels in Cream Sauce

Fresh mussels are available year round, but they have the most flavor during the cold months: a good reason for trying mussels in cream sauce.

Serves 6

6–8 dozen fresh mussels
1 small leek
2 stalks celery
1 bunch fresh or
2 teaspoons dried parsley
small bunch fresh or
1 teaspoon dried dill
1–2 sprigs fresh or
½ teaspoon dried thyme
1 bay leaf
1–2 cloves garlic
3 tablespoons butter
freshly ground black pepper
1 cup dry white wine
6 tablespoons water
1 onion
1½ cups light cream
1 egg yolk
salt
pinch sugar
pinch of cayenne pepper

Preparation time: 1 hour

Scrub and clean the mussel shells thoroughly in several changes of cold water. Discard any which are already open. Remove the beards by holding them firmly between thumb and knife blade and scraping them off carefully. Place the mussels in a large saucepan.

Trim the leek and celery. Cut the leek into fine rings and the celery into thin slices. Put the leek in a sieve and rinse to remove any grit that might remain. Place the leek and celery on top of the mussels in the pan. Chop the parsley coarsely; pluck the dill and thyme apart. Place all the herbs with the bay leaf in the pan.

Peel the cloves of garlic and cut them into quarters lengthwise. Place them on top of the mussels with a very small pat of the butter and a generous amount of freshly ground black pepper. Mix the wine and water and pour it into the pan. Cover and bring to a boil. Steam the mussels for 5–10 minutes, shaking the pan frequently so that all the mussels get an equal amount of heat to open.

Place a large sieve or colander over a bowl or pan and pour the mussels and the liquid into it. Strain the mussel liquid, which will have drained through into the bowl or pan, through a paper coffee filter or a fine sieve to remove any grains of sand and pieces of vegetable. Reserve the liquid. Remove the mussels from their shells, using empty mussel shells as tweezers. Discard any mussels which are still shut. Set the mussels aside.

Peel the onion and chop finely. Heat the rest of the butter in a saucepan and fry the onion until it is soft and golden. Stir in the reserved mussel liquid and cream, increase the heat and boil down the sauce until it is thick and creamy. Beat the egg yolk in a cup and stir in a little of the cream sauce. Remove the pan from the heat and stir in the egg mixture when the sauce is no longer simmering.

Place the mussels in the sauce, return the pan to a gentle heat and let the mussels warm through. The sauce should on no account be allowed to boil. Season to taste with salt, pepper, sugar and cayenne pepper. Sprinkle with the tiniest amount of cayenne pepper and serve immediately. Fresh French bread or black bread with butter go well with this dish. Serve the same wine as used in the sauce, or beer.

1 **Removing the beards.** The black strand known as a "beard" must be removed. Hold it firmly between thumb and knife blade and scrape off carefully.

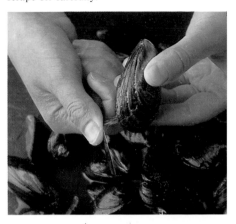

2 **Adding the liquid.** Mix the wine and the water and pour it over the mussels. Bring to a boil in the covered pan, then steam until the shells open.

3 **Draining the mussels.** Place a large colander or sieve over a pan or bowl and tip the mussels and the liquid into it. Allow the mussels to drain throughly.

4 **Extracting the mussels** from their shells. Use empty mussel shells as tweezers to pull the mussels from their shells. Discard any mussels which remain closed.

Bass in Puff Pastry

If you would like to serve something really unusual, try this delicious recipe for bass, stuffed with vegetables, herbs and shrimp and baked whole in puff pastry. It requires time and patience, but is worth it.

Serves 6

I sea bass, weighing
1¾–2 lb, dressed
1¼ lb puff pastry,
fresh or frozen
1 lemon
salt
freshly ground white pepper
2 stalks celery
1 small leek
1 sprig fresh thyme
2 sprigs fresh tarragon
1 bunch fresh parsley
2 tablespoons butter
3 tablespoons dry white wine
2 hard-cooked eggs
½ cup cooked shelled shrimp
3–4 tablespoons soft bread crumbs
2 eggs
pinch of cayenne pepper

To thaw: 30 minutes
Preparation time: 2 hours

Rinse the fish throughly under cold running water and pat dry. If using frozen pastry, separate the sheets of pastry and place them on the working surface to thaw. Rinse the lemon in hot water, then dry well. Grate a little of the rind and squeeze out the juice. Sprinkle the fish inside and out with a little lemon juice and season with salt and pepper. Put on one side while you prepare the filling.

Trim the celery and leek and chop finely. Rinse the herbs, shake them dry and chop finely. Melt the butter in a small skillet and fry the celery and leek over a moderate heat, stirring all the time, until they are tender. Add the wine and simmer until the liquid has evaporated. Remove the pan from the heat and allow to cool.

Shell the hard-cooked eggs and chop them. Chop the shrimp coarsely. Mix the chopped eggs and shrimp with the cooled vegetables. Add 2 tablespoons of the bread crumbs, half the egg and the herbs, and season to taste with salt, pepper, cayenne pepper and grated lemon rind.

Preheat the oven to 400 F.

Place one-third of the pastry on a floured surface. Roll out into a rectangle that is large enough for the fish. Sprinkle the remaining bread crumbs on the center of the pastry in the shape of the fish.

Pat the fish dry once again and stuff with some of the prepared filling. Lay the fish on the pastry. Mold the rest of the filling into the shape of a fish head on the pastry. Trim off the excess pastry around the fish and "head", leaving a margin about 1 inch wide. Separate the remaining

egg and beat the white and yolk separately. Brush the pastry margin around the fish with egg white.

Take the next third of pastry, roll it out and place over the fish. Press this pastry lid carefully onto the base and seal the margins using a fork. Remove any excess pastry with a pastry cutter or knife. Using two large knives or spatulas, lift the pastry-wrapped fish onto a baking sheet which has been sprinkled with cold water.

Put the remaining third of pastry and the pastry trimmings on top of one another – do not knead them together – and roll out the pastry on a floured surface. Cut out small decorative rounds with a pastry cutter. Brush the fish all over with beaten egg yolk, then lay the pastry rounds on the fish to represent scales. Brush the pastry frequently with egg yolk so that the "scales" stick on firmly. When it is ready, brush the fish with egg yolk for the last time.

Place the baking sheet in the heated oven and bake for 30–40 minutes. Remove from the oven and let stand for 10 minutes before serving.

1 **Shaping the fish.** Place the stuffed bass on the pastry and mold the rest of the filling into the shape of a fish head. Remove the excess pastry, leaving a margin.

2 **Trimming the edges.** Seal the margins together with a fork and remove the excess pastry. Lift the fish onto a baking sheet which has been sprinkled with cold water.

3 **Making the fish scales.** Place the pastry rounds on the fish to resemble fish scales. Brush the pastry frequently with beaten egg yolk so that the scales stick firmly.

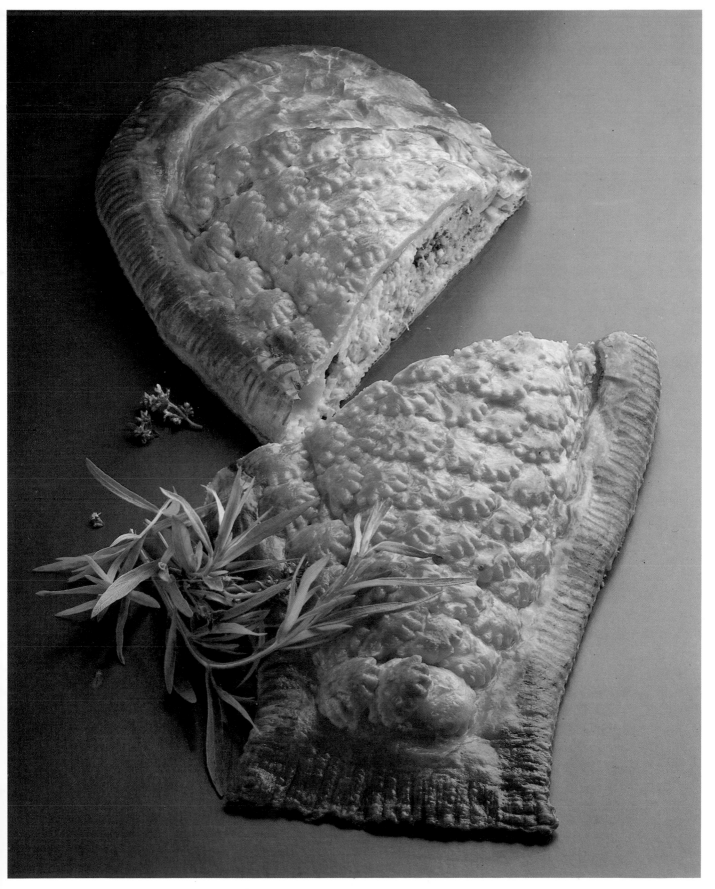

Salmon Fillets in Tarragon Sauce

This beautiful dish of salmon fillets in creamy tarragon sauce deserves a place of honor on any special menu.

Serves 6

2 lb fresh salmon,
from the tail, in 2 fillets
juice ½ lemon
salt
1 onion
2 tablespoons butter
¼ cup dry white wine
¼ cup dry vermouth
6 tablespoons heavy cream
4 sprigs fresh or
½ teaspoon dried tarragon
5 tablespoons vegetable oil
freshly ground white pepper

For the stock:
¾ lb fish bones
and trimmings
1¼ cups water
1 onion
3 sprigs fresh parsley
1 small sprig fresh thyme
1 teaspoon lemon juice
6 tablespoons dry white wine
½ bay leaf

Preparation time: 1 hour

Rinse the fish bones and trimmings under cold running water and place in a saucepan. Cover with the water and bring to a boil, skimming off any scum which rises to the surface.

Meanwhile, peel the onion and chop finely. Rinse the parsley and thyme and shake dry. Add the onion and herbs to the fish stock together with the lemon juice, white wine and bay leaf. Simmer over a gentle heat for 15–20 minutes, then strain through a fine sieve or paper coffee filter.

To prepare the salmon, lay the two pieces on a wooden board and slice them both in half horizontally with a very sharp knife to make four flat pieces of equal size. Sprinkle both sides of the fish with lemon juice and salt. Place each slice of salmon between two sheets of oiled wax paper and pat gently with the flat side of a carving knife to flatten. Set aside.

Peel the onion and chop finely. Melt the butter in a saucepan and fry the onion gently until it is soft and golden. Add the strained fish stock, white wine and dry vermouth. Bring to a boil, then strain through a sieve and return to the pan.

Pour the cream into the strained liquid, stirring all the time, then bring back to a boil and boil briskly to reduce until the sauce is creamy in consistency. Rinse the tarragon, shake dry and cut half of the leaves into thin strips. Place the strips in the sauce. Keep the sauce warm (but do not allow to boil).

Heat the oil in a skillet and fry each slice of salmon on both sides for 30 seconds. Place for a moment on paper towels to drain off any excess oil, then season with a little pepper and serve with the sauce. Garnish with the remaining tarragon.

1 **Dividing the salmon.** Place the two pieces of fish on a wooden board and cut each in half horizontally with a very sharp knife. Season with lemon juice and salt.

2 **Flattening the slices.** Place each slice of fish between two sheets of oiled wax paper. Pat gently with the side of a knife blade to flatten, but do not break the flesh.

3 **Reducing the sauce.** Pour in the cream, stirring constantly, and boil down the sauce in the open pan until it is creamy in consistency. Add the tarragon.

4 **Frying the salmon.** Heat the oil in a skillet and fry the salmon for 30 seconds on each side. Remove from the pan and drain briefly on paper towels.

Snails with Chablis Butter

Snails in Chablis butter are a perennial favorite. Serve them with French bread and the same wine as used in the recipe.

---

36 snail shells
36 canned snails
2–3 shallots
1–2 cloves garlic
10 tablespoons butter
6 tablespoons Chablis or
other dry white wine
1 bunch fresh parsley
1 sprig fresh or
¼ teaspoon dried thyme
salt
freshly ground white pepper
Worcestershire sauce

Preparation time: 30 minutes

Preheat the oven to 425°F. If necessary, rinse out the snail shells with boiling water and turn them upside down to dry. Drain the snails, reserving the liquid in the cans. Put a few drops of the reserved liquid into each snail shell followed by a snail. Press each one lightly into the shell so that there is enough room for the Chablis butter.

Peel the shallots and garlic and chop them so finely that they are almost a pulp. Melt 1 tablespoon of the butter in a small pan and add the shallots and garlic. Fry over a gentle heat, stirring constantly, until they are soft and transparent. As soon as the mixture starts to take on color, add the rest of the liquid from the canned snails. Turn the heat up high, add the Chablis and let the liquid boil down until only about 2 tablespoons remain. Remove the pan from the heat and let cool.

Rinse the parsley and thyme, shake dry and chop as finely as possible. Beat the rest of the butter until it is pale and creamy, then mix in the cooled shallot mixture and the chopped herbs. Blend everything well together and season to taste with salt, pepper and a few drops of Worcestershire sauce so that the butter is piquant in flavor. Using a knife, seal the snails in the shells with the butter. All the snails should be generously covered with the butter. Press it well into the shells so that the snails really are enhanced by the flavor of the Chablis during cooking.

Arrange the snails on ovenproof escargot dishes and place them in the heated oven. Bake them for about 5 minutes or until the butter begins to foam up in the shells; they will then be really hot right through. Remove from the oven and serve immediately. Snails taste their best when they are served steaming hot.

1 **Filling the shells.** Put a few drops of the liquid from the cans of snails into each shell and then a snail. Press the snail lightly into the shell so that there is room for the Chablis butter.

2 **Reducing the liquid.** Add the rest of the liquid from the can of snails, then stir in the Chablis. Boil until reduced to about 2 tablespoons of liquid. Allow to cool.

3 **Sealing the shells.** Using a knife, press the Chablis butter into each shell so that the snail inside is generously covered. Place the snails on ovenproof escargot dishes and bake.

Our tip

If you do not have escargot dishes, fill a casserole or baking dish with a layer of coarse salt about $\frac{3}{4}$ inch thick and stand the shells on it. Baked in this way, they will not fall over and can be brought to the table on the bed of salt.

Finnish Fish Pie

Surprise your friends with this unusual Finnish fish pie when you next invite them for an informal party. Traditionally, it should be served with a cool beer and an ice cold aquavit.

Serves 8

3¾ cups light rye flour
1¾ cups all-purpose flour
salt
2–2½ cups water
1 cup (½ lb) butter
2 trout, each weighing
½ lb, dressed
2 small perch or herrings,
each weighing ½ lb, dressed
1 lb fresh salmon
freshly ground black pepper
juice 1 lemon
1 lb fresh pork fat

Preparation time: 1 hour
Baking time: about 2½ hours

Sift the rye and all-purpose flours and 1 teaspoon salt into a large bowl. Make a hollow in the flour and pour in the water. Cut 5 tablespoons of the butter into small pieces and place the pieces around the edges of the flour. Mix the ingredients together, stirring from the middle to the sides with a wooden spoon until the dough is very firm. When it is impossible to stir it any longer, remove from the bowl and knead it with the hands until it is entirely smooth. Shape the dough into a ball and dust with flour. Return to the bowl and cover with a cloth. Set aside.

Preheat the oven to 475°F. Rinse the fish under cold running water and pat dry. Remove the backbone and any other large bones; the smaller ones will become soft during the long cooking process. (The Finns do not remove any bones.) Scale the salmon if necessary. Cut all the fish into strips about the thickness of a finger and season to taste with salt, pepper and lemon juice. Cut the pork into equal-sized strips and season to taste with salt and pepper.

Knead the dough again. Dredge a sheet of aluminum foil with flour and place the dough on it. Roll it out into a large round about ½ inch thick. Place the seasoned fish and pork strips in layers in the middle of the dough round. Cut 2 tablespoons of the remaining butter into pieces and dot over the filling. Using the foil to lift the dough, pull the edges up and wrap them over the filling. Release the foil and with wet hands smooth over the edges so that there are no gaps in the surface.

Line a baking sheet with foil. Melt the remaining butter and brush a little over the foil. Place the fish pie on the foil and shape it into a hemisphere with wet hands. Wet a knife and smooth over the surface so that it is quite even. Place the baking sheet in the heated oven and bake for 1 hour. Fold the foil over the pie to protect the surface and reduce the heat to 350°F. Bake for a further 1½ hours. About 15 minutes before the end of the cooking time, remove the foil from the top of the pie and brush the pastry a few times with melted butter.

Remove the pie from the oven. Lay a piece of wet wax paper over the top and cover it with a cloth so that the crust cannot become hard. The pie can be served immediately or allowed to cool and served warm or cold. To serve, cut a round lid in the top of the pie. Cut each person a portion of the crust, over which they should then pour some of the remaining melted butter and spoon a portion of the pie filling on top of the crust.

1 **Mixing the dough.** Stirring from the center towards the edges, mix the dough together until it is very firm. When it becomes impossible to stir, knead it with your hands.

2 **Filling the pie.** Place the seasoned fish and pork strips in layers in the center of the dough round. Dot with 2 tablespoons of the remaining butter, cut into pieces.

3 **Smoothing the surface.** Pull the edges of the dough round up over the filling. Wet a knife and smooth over the surface of the pie. Bake on the bottom shelf of the oven.

4 **Opening the pie.** Serve the pie hot, warm or cold. Cut a round lid in the top with a sharp knife and serve each person a portion of crust. Serve with the rest of the melted butter and a portion of the filling.

Liver Pâté

This excellent pâté can be presented as a first course; served with thin slices of French bread, it can also be a delicious hors d'oeuvre for special guests.

Serves 8

1¾ veal liver
¾ lb fresh pork fat
2 shallots
1 clove garlic
2–3 anchovy fillets
1½ stale rolls
3 sprigs fresh or
½ teaspoon dried thyme
2 sprigs fresh or
¼ teaspoon dried rosemary
1 sprig fresh or
¼ teaspoon dried sage
pinch ground allspice
pinch ground ginger
2 bay leaves
1 orange
2 tablespoons Cognac or port
1 egg
1 egg yolk
¾ cup light cream
1½–2 teaspoons salt
1 (½-oz) can truffles (optional)
2 tablespoons green peppercorns
1 lb salt pork,
thinly sliced, or thin
bacon slices

To marinate: 4–24 hours
Preparation time: 2 hours
To cool: 4–24 hours

Prepare the liver by removing any skin, tubes or sinews and cutting it into strips. Cut the pork fat into strips of roughly the same size. Place the pork and liver strips in a large bowl.

Peel the shallots and garlic and chop finely. Cut the anchovy fillets in half. Remove the crust from the rolls thinly by grating it off. Cut the rolls into small cubes. Rinse the herbs and shake dry. Put a sprig of thyme and a sprig of rosemary aside for use later. Strip the leaves from the rest of the herbs and add them to the bowl together with the shallots, garlic, anchovy fillets and bread cubes. Season with allspice and ginger and place a bay leaf on top.

Rinse the orange in hot water and dry thoroughly. Grate the rind. Cut the orange in half and squeeze the juice from one half. Sprinkle the grated rind and juice over the contents of the bowl and add the Cognac or port. Beat the egg, egg yolk and cream together, pour over the other ingredients and mix thoroughlu. Cover the bowl with plastic wrap or foil and leave to marinate in the refrigerator overnight or for at least 4 hours.

Preheat the oven to 325°F. Remove the bay leaf. Grind the ingredients as finely as possible, or place in portions in a blender or food processor and reduce to a purée. Return the mixture to the bowl and place on a bed of ice cubes. Stir it with a wooden spoon until it is smooth and shiny. Season to taste with salt.

Drain the truffle, reserving the liquid from the can. Chop the truffle finely. Stir into the mixture together with the liquid from the can and the green peppercorns. Put the bowl in a cool place while preparing the terrine.

Line a large 1½-quart terrine with about four-fifths of the thinly sliced salt pork or bacon slices, arranging it so that a little hangs over the edges of the terrine. Spoon the pâté mixture into the terrine and smooth the surface. Arrange the rest of the salt pork or bacon slices on top. Place the rest of the herbs and the second bay leaf on the fat. Cover the terrine and stand it in a baking pan. Pour enough boiling water into the pan to come halfway up the sides of the terrine. Place in the heated oven and cook for about 1 hour 10 minutes.

Take the terrine from the oven, remove the lid and leave it to cool. Weight the pâté overnight, if you like, but this is not really necessary.

1 **Marinating the ingredients.** Beat the egg, egg yolk and cream together, pour over the ingredients and mix thoroughly. Cover the dish and leave for at least 4 hours.

2 **Preparing the pâté mixture.** Place the ground or puréed mixture in a bowl and stand it on a bed of ice cubes. Stir the mixture with a wooden spoon until it is smooth and shiny.

3 **Seasoning the mixture.** Add salt to taste followed by the truffle, with the liquid from the can, and the green peppercorns. Keep the mixture cool while preparing the terrine.

4 **Lining the terrine.** Line the terrine with about four-fifths of the salt pork or bacon so that a little hangs over the edge of the dish. Spoon the mixture into the dish.

Our tip

The pâté will cut more easily if it is weighted after cooking. Lay a suitably sized board or plate on top of the pâté and use a large can or a pan filled with water as a weight. Leave overnight before serving.

Saltimbocca alla Romana

This famous Italian dish – veal cutlets with fresh sage leaves and Parma ham – is well named. "Saltimbocca" literally translated means "jump in the mouth."

Serves 4

8 veal cutlets, each
weighing about 3 oz
16 leaves fresh sage
freshly ground white pepper
8 thin slices Parma ham
or prosciutto
5 tablespoons butter
6 tablespoons dry white wine
salt

Preparation time: 25 minutes

Dry both sides of the veal cutlets with paper towels and place each one between two sheets of wax paper on the work surface. Beat the cutlets with a meat mallet or rolling pin until they are twice as large as before and half as thick. Do not break the meat fibers. Remove the paper and press out any unevenness in the veal with the ball of the thumb.

Rinse the sage leaves under cold running water and dry very thoroughly on paper towels or a dish towel. Grind a little pepper over the cutlets and lay two sage leaves on top of each. Remove any excess fat from the Parma ham or prosciutto and lay a slice over the sage leaves on each cutlet. Use wooden toothpicks to fasten the ham securely to the veal.

Melt 3–4 tablespoons of the butter in a large skillet and fry the cutlets, two or three at a time, for about 3 minutes on each side. Fry the side with the ham last. Remove the cutlets from the skillet as they are ready and keep warm. When all are cooked, pour the wine into the skillet and loosen any meat sediments from the bottom and sides of the pan with a wooden spoon. Reduce the liquid by boiling rapidly until it is of a syrupy consistency. Season to taste with salt and pepper. Remove the pan from the heat.

Cut the rest of the butter into small pieces and beat them into the sauce, one piece at a time. Season the cutlets lightly on both sides with salt and pepper and remove the toothpicks. Place the cutlets on a heated serving dish and pour the sauce over them. Serve with French bread or a risotto.

1 **Flattening the cutlets.** Beat the cutlets between sheets of wax paper until they are twice as large as before and half as thick, then press out any unevenness with the thumb.

2 **Covering the cutlets with ham.** Place a slice of ham on each seasoned cutlet so that the sage leaves are covered. Secure with two wooden toothpicks.

3 **Frying the saltimbocca.** Melt the butter in a skillet and fry the cutlets for 3 minutes on each side, frying the ham side last. Remove from the pan and keep warm while making the sauce.

Our tip

The type of ham used is important. It must be a mild, air-dried ham such as Parma or San Daniele. Smoked ham is far too strong in flavor and should not be used. The wine, however, can be varied. In Italy Marsala wine is often used instead of white wine and is excellent with the veal.

Osso Buco

Osso buco – in English, braised shank of veal – is typically Italian. Pasta, risotto with cheese or Italian bread can be served with it.

Serves 8

2 onions
3 carrots
½ stalk celery
3–4 cloves garlic
8 meaty pieces of veal shank,
  each weighing ½ lb
salt
freshly ground black pepper
½ cup flour
4–5 tablespoons olive oil
2 tablespoons butter
6 tablespoons dry white wine
4 large ripe tomatoes
½–1 cup hot beef broth
small bunch fresh basil
2 sprigs fresh or
½ teaspoon dried thyme
2 bunches fresh parsley
1 small bay leaf
½–1 lemon

Preparation time: 2 hours

Peel and finely chop the onions and carrots. Trim the celery, removing any hard strings, and cut lengthwise into quarters and then across into very thin slices. Peel the garlic and chop finely. Preheat the oven to 350°F.

Wipe the meat with a damp cloth to remove any tiny pieces of bone. Season with salt and pepper, rubbing the seasoning into the surface of the meat. Tie up the pieces of shank firmly with heavy string. First bind the string around the pieces of veal, then tie them up like small parcels. Dust with the flour and press it lightly onto the meat. Heat the oil in a large skillet. Add the pieces of veal shank, a few at a time, and brown on all sides. Remove from the heat.

Melt the butter in a large flameproof casserole and add the onions, carrots, celery and half the garlic. Fry the vegetables for 10–15 minutes or until they are soft and golden. Remove the casserole from the heat and place the well-browned veal shank pieces on top of the vegetables.

Carefully pour off the excess fat from the skillet, but retain the meat juices. Pour a little of the wine into the pan, stirring briskly to loosen any meat sediments, and bring to a boil. Boil to reduce the liquid to about half.

Meanwhile, scald the tomatoes in boiling water for 10 seconds, then peel and remove the core and any hard pieces of green stem. Cut the tomatoes in half so that all seed chambers are visible and, taking half a tomato at a time in the palm of your hand, squeeze gently until the seeds fall out. Discard these, chop the tomatoes and add to the casserole. Pour the liquid from the skillet over the contents of the casserole and add the remaining wine and the broth. The meat and vegetables should be almost covered with liquid. Add more if necessary.

Rinse the basil, thyme and parsley in cold water and shake dry. Chop the thyme and basil finely. Place the chopped herbs together with half the parsley sprigs and the bay leaf in the casserole. Season generously with salt and pepper. Cover the casserole, place in the heated oven and cook for 1 hour to 1 hour 10 minutes.

To make the seasoning mixture

(gremolata), chop the remaining parsley finely. Rinse the lemon with hot water, dry thoroughly and grate the rind. Mix the parsley and lemon rind with the rest of the finely chopped garlic.

When the meat is ready, remove the string. Discard the parsley sprigs and bay leaf. Serve the meat and vegetables with the gremolata sprinkled over it. The dish should be served straight from the oven or it will lose some of its flavor.

Our tip

In Italy braised shanks of veal are served with "riso giallo" – yellow rice – a risotto seasoned with saffron. The special rice called "avorio" that the Italians use for risotto can be obtained in some markets. It is prepared as follows: melt some butter in a pan and fry a peeled and diced onion. Add the rice and fry gently in the butter, then add small quantities of broth or wine as required until the rice is tender. Towards the end of cooking time, dissolve a tiny pinch of crumbled saffron threads in a little broth or water and stir it into the rice.

1 Tying up the meat. Tie a piece of heavy string around each seasoned piece of shank so that they resemble small parcels. Dredge with flour and press it onto the meat.

2 Frying the ingredients. Brown the meat well on all sides in the oil in a skillet. Fry the vegetables and half the garlic in the butter in a flameproof casserole.

3 Adding the wine and broth. The ingredients should be almost covered with liquid. The amount of liquid required will depend on the size of the casserole.

4 Making the gremolata. Chop the remaining parsley finely, grate the lemon rind over it and mix with the rest of the finely chopped garlic. Sprinkle over the osso buco just before serving.

Vitello Tonnato

Italian cuisine is famous for its many delightful veal recipes. This braised veal dish with its spicy tuna fish sauce is one of the best and tastes particularly good on a warm summer evening.

Serves 4

1 boneless veal roast,
weighing 1¾ lb
(rump or boned rolled leg)
1 onion
1 carrot
2 stalks celery, or ¼ celeriac
1 bunch fresh parsley
2 bay leaves
6 white peppercorns
¾ cup dry white wine
2 cups chicken broth
1 (7-oz) can Italian tuna fish in oil
5 anchovy fillets
1 egg yolk
6 tablespoons olive oil
1 lemon
salt
freshly ground white pepper
2 tablespoons small capers

Preparation time: 1½ hours
Cooling time: 3–4 hours

Wipe the meat with a damp cloth and tie into shape, if necessary. Place in a saucepan which is just large enough to hold it so that it does not "swim" when the liquid is added. Peel the onion and carrot and chop coarsely. Trim the celery, remove any tough threads and cut into slices, or peel and dice the celeriac. Rinse the parsley and shake it dry. Place the vegetables, bay leaves, peppercorns and three-quarters of the parsley in the pan with the meat.

Mix the wine with the chicken broth and pour it over the meat. Shake the pan to distribute the liquid and add sufficient cold water to cover the meat. Cover the pan and bring to a boil over a high heat. Reduce the heat and simmer gently for about 1 hour or until the veal is tender. Remove from the heat. Remove ¾ cup of the stock for the sauce, strain it and set aside. Leave the veal to cool in the remaining stock. The cooling process will take 3–4 hours.

Drain the tuna and anchovy fillets reserving the oil from the cans. Place a small portion of tuna and two anchovy fillets in a mortar and pound to a pulp with the pestle, or use a food processor. Pass the pulp through a fine sieve. Repeat with the remaining tuna and anchovy fillets. Set aside.

To make the thick mayonnaise base for the sauce, beat the egg yolk with a balloon whisk until it is thick and frothy. Add the oil, drop by drop, beating all the time until the mayonnaise is thick and creamy. Cut the lemon in half and squeeze the juice from one half. Mix the juice with the fish pulp, a few drops of the reserved fish oil and a little of the reserved strained stock. Stir into the mayonnaise. Add

enough of the remaining strained stock to give the sauce the consistency of light cream. Season to taste with salt and pepper and stir in the drained capers.

Remove the veal from the stock and drain well. Slice it thinly and arrange it on a serving platter so that the slices overlap one another. Pour the sauce over the meat. Slice the rest of the lemon and use as a garnish with the remaining parsley. Fresh white bread and dry white wine go well with this dish.

1 **Adding the liquid.** Pour the white wine and chicken broth over the meat and vegetables in the pan and add sufficient cold water to cover the meat. Cover the pan and bring to a boil.

2 **Pounding the fish.** Pound small quantities of tuna and anchovy to a smooth pulp in a mortar with a pestle, then pass through a fine sieve. Set the pulp aside.

3 **Preparing the mayonnaise.** Beat the egg yolk until it is frothy. Add the oil drop by drop, continuing to beat until the mixture is thick and creamy. Add the remaining sauce ingredients.

Our tip

If there are any leftovers, they can be used to make other dishes. The meat can be cut into thin strips and mixed with diced cooked artichoke hearts. Serve on a bed of lettuce topped with any remaining tuna sauce. A few diced tomatoes make a colorful garnish. The veal could also be combined with pieces of celery, avocado and chopped walnuts. Serve these ingredients with radicchio (red lettuce), fennel or corn salad to give the dish a summery freshness.

Fegato alla Veneziana

Calves' liver Venetian style is not a dish that can be made quickly; the onions need to be stewed slowly in butter and wine in order to develop the slightly sweet flavor that harmonizes so well with sautéed liver.

1¼ lb calves' liver
2 onions
¼ cup olive oil
2 tablespoons butter
1 bunch fresh parsley
6 tablespoons dry white wine
salt
freshly ground black pepper
little wine vinegar

Preparation time: 1 hour

Remove any skin from the liver by carefully lifting it up at the edge with a sharp knife and then pulling it off by hand. Hold the piece of liver firmly on the work surface with the other hand while carrying out this operation. Cut off any sinewy pieces and remove the tubes by cutting around them with a thin, sharp knife and pulling them out. The liver will not become hard and tough during frying if time and trouble is taken beforehand with the preparation. Cut the liver into slices 1½–2 inches thick, then cut these slices into strips about as thick as a finger. They should all be about the same size to ensure even cooking.

Peel the onions and slice thinly. Heat the oil and butter in a large skillet and fry the onions gently, stirring them from time to time, until they are soft and transparent. Do not let them brown.

Meanwhile, rinse the parsley, shake it dry and chop finely.

When the onions just start to become golden in color, add the wine and continue cooking as before, stirring frequently, until all the liquid has evaporated.

Increase the heat and push the onions to one side of the pan. Place the liver in the hot fat, a few strips at a time, and fry them quickly, turning frequently, until browned on all sides. Push those that are ready to the side of the pan before adding the next portion. When all are ready, mix the liver strips with the onions and season to taste with salt, pepper and a dash of wine vinegar. Stir in the chopped parsley and serve immediately as liver becomes hard and tough if it has to stand. Serve with fresh French bread or boiled rice.

1 **Removing the skin from the liver.** Carefully lift the skin with the point of a knife and then pull it off by hand. Cut off any sinewy pieces and tubes using a thin, sharp knife.

2 **Cutting the liver into strips.** Cut the liver into slices $1\frac{1}{2}$–2 inches thick and the slices into strips about as wide as a finger. The strips must be of the same size to ensure even cooking.

3 **Frying the liver.** Push the onions to the side of the pan and place the liver, a few strips at a time, in the hot fat. Fry quickly until browned on all sides, turning frequently.

Veal Kidneys in Cognac Sauce

Tender veal kidneys in creamy Cognac sauce is a dish that is worth serving more often.

Serves 4

1¼ lb veal kidneys
2 shallots
2 tablespoons butter
1 tablespoon vegetable oil
2 tablespoons brandy or Cognac
3 tablespoons dry white wine
1 cup heavy cream
salt
freshly ground black pepper
pinch sugar
small bunch fresh parsley
1 teaspoon green peppercorns

Preparation time: 30 minutes

Rinse the kidneys under cold running water, pat dry and halve lengthwise. Clean the kidneys by removing any skin and fat and cutting out the cores. Do this carefully so that the kidneys keep their shape. Take a very sharp knife and cut the kidney halves carefully into slices ¼ inch thick. Dry the slices on paper towels. Peel and finely chop the shallots.

Heat the butter and oil in a skillet and fry the kidney slices, a few at a time, for about 1 minute, stirring all the time. As each portion is ready, place in a sieve with a plate underneath to catch the juices.

When all the kidney pieces are ready, fry the shallot in the hot fat, stirring all the time, until it is soft and golden. Holding the shallot firmly in the pan with a spatula or spoon, pour off the excess fat. Add 1 tablespoon of brandy and the wine to the pan and bring to a boil, scraping up any meat sediment sticking to the bottom and sides of the pan. Stir in the cream, and season to taste with salt, pepper and sugar. Boil down over a high heat until the sauce has reduced and is creamy in consistency.

Meanwhile, rinse the parsley, shake it dry and chop finely. Drain the liquid from the green peppercorns and crush them a little, if desired.

Remove the pan from the heat and stir in the juices from the kidneys, the parsley and peppercorns. Fold in the kidney slices. Return the pan to gentle heat and warm through. Do not boil or the kidneys will become hard and tough. Add the rest of the brandy and serve immediately with a tossed green salad and boiled potatoes or boiled rice.

1 **Preparing the kidneys.** Halve the kidneys. Remove any skin or fat and cut out the cores, using a sharp knife. Do this carefully so that the kidneys keep their shape.

2 **Slicing the kidneys.** Using a sharp knife, cut each kidney half into slices about ¼ inch thick. Dry the slices on both sides on paper towels.

3 **Pouring off the fat.** Holding the fried shallot back firmly with a spatula, pour the excess fat from the skillet. Add 1 tablespoon of the Cognac and the wine.

4 **Adding the kidneys.** When the sauce has been reduced sufficiently, add the kidneys and juices that have drained from them, the parsley and green peppercorns.

Our tip

It is not necessary to soak tender young veal kidneys before cooking them. Only kidneys from mature animals require soaking, to remove their strong odor. It is very important not to boil the sauce again once the kidneys have been added. If it boils, the kidneys will be hard and tough and lose their delicate aroma.

Bitki Carnot

Russian cooks often create particularly appetizing delicacies out of so-called "everyday dishes". In this case, meatballs (bitki) made fron finely ground veal are stuffed with pâté de foie gras, coated thickly with béchamel sauce and bread crumbs and deep fried.

Serves 4

---

3 slices stale white bread
small bunch fresh parsley
1 lb ground veal
2 eggs plus 1 egg yolk
salt
freshly ground white pepper
1 teaspoon green peppercorns
1 (3-oz) can
pâté de foie gras
1½ quarts veal or
beef broth
1 slice or about 2 oz cooked ham
1 small onion
2 tablespoons butter
¼ cup flour
1 cup hot milk
grated nutmeg
oil for deep frying
1⅓ cups dry bread crumbs

Preparation time: 1½ hours
Cooling time: 2–3 hours

Remove the crusts from the bread. Tear the bread into pieces and place in a bowl. Cover with lukewarm water and leave to soak for 10 minutes. Meanwhile, rinse the parsley, shake it dry and chop finely.

Put the ground veal in a bowl and add the chopped parsley, one of the eggs, salt and pepper to taste and the drained green peppercorns. Squeeze the excess liquid from the bread, and add to the bowl. Mix the ingredients together well, kneading until the mixture is very smooth. Adjust the seasoning if necessary. Shape into balls about 1½ inches in diameter.

Make a small depression in the side of each meatball and place a suitably sized piece of pâté in it. Close the meat around the pâté and roll the meatball between the palms of your hands until it is smooth and round again.

Bring the broth to a boil in a large saucepan. When it is boiling, place a few meatballs in it. Reduce the heat and simmer for 5–8 minutes. Remove the meatballs with a slotted spoon. Bring the broth to a boil again and repeat the process until all the meatballs have been cooked. Drain them thoroughly and put aside to cool.

Dice the ham. Peel the onion and chop very finely. Melt the butter in a saucepan and fry the ham and the onion until they are soft. Sprinkle the flour over them and stir until the mixture becomes frothy. Gradually add the milk, stirring all the time, and simmer until the sauce resembles a thick paste. Season to taste with salt, pepper and nutmeg and remove from the heat. Beat a little of the sauce with the egg yolk in a cup, then stir into the remaining sauce in the pan. Leave to cool.

Heat the oil in a deep fat fryer to 350°F. Place the bread crumbs on a plate. Coat the meatballs thickly with the sauce, then roll in the bread crumbs until they are completely and evenly covered. Set aside so that the bread crumbs can dry on the surface.

Beat the remaining egg lightly in a shallow dish. Dip the meatballs in the beaten egg, then roll in the bread crumbs again. Press the crumbs lightly onto the surface. Deep fry, a few meatballs at a time, in the hot oil for 4–6 minutes. Remove with a slotted spoon and drain on paper towels. Serve very hot.

1 **Filling the meatballs.** Make a small depression in the side of each meatball and fill with a piece of pâté. Close the meat around the pâté and roll into a smooth ball again.

2 **Cooking the meatballs.** When the broth is boiling, place the meatballs in it, a few at a time. Simmer for 5–8 minutes, then drain and allow to cool. Meanwhile, make the sauce.

3 **Coating the meatballs.** Coat the meatballs with sauce and roll in the bread crumbs. Let the crumbs dry on the surface, then dip in beaten egg and roll in bread crumbs again.

Our tip

Bitki carnot may also be served cold, but they must be thoroughly drained of oil after frying. Remove from the oil with a slotted spoon, let the oil drain off and then place on a thick layer of paper towels. Pat dry with another piece of paper towel.

Beef Wellington

Sufficient time for careful preparation is absolutely essential for the success of this version of filet de boeuf en croûte.

Serves 4

---

1 piece beef tenderloin,
weighing about 1 lb
2 tablespoons vegetable oil
salt
freshly ground black pepper
¾ lb frozen puff pastry
¼ lb cooked ham
2 onions
1 clove garlic
1 carrot
1 leek
1 stalk celery
½ lb button mushrooms
1 bunch fresh parsley
1 tomato
2 tablespoons butter
¼ cup port or Madeira
⅛ teaspoon dried rosemary
⅛ teaspoon dried thyme
1 (3-oz) can pâté de foie gras
2 tablespoons soft bread crumbs
1 egg plus 1 egg yolk

To thaw: 20 minutes
Preparation time: 2 hours

Pat the meat dry with paper towels. Heat the oil in a skillet and brown the meat on all sides over a high heat for about 10 minutes. Remove from the pan. Season the meat on all sides with salt and pepper and put aside to cool.

While the meat is cooling, place the sheet of puff pastry on the work surface and leave it to thaw. Remove any fat from the ham. Peel the onions, garlic and carrot. Trim the leek and celery. Clean the mushrooms. Dice the ham and vegetables very finely. Rinse the parsley, shake it dry and chop finely. Scald the tomato in boiling water for 10 seconds, then peel and remove the core and any pieces of hard stem. Cut in half so that all seed chambers are visible and, taking half a tomato at a time in the palm of your hand, squeeze gently until the seeds fall out, then discard them. Chop the tomato flesh finely.

Melt the butter in the clean skillet and fry the ham, shaking the pan all the time so that it does not brown. Add the prepared vegetables and cook, stirring constantly, until they are soft and any vegetable juices have evaporated. Stir in the port or Madeira and cook until the wine has evaporated. Turn the mixture into a bowl and set aside to cool.

Add the herbs to the mixture with the pâté, bread crumbs and whole egg. Season to taste with salt and pepper and stir until the mixture is well blended.

Roll out the sheet of puff pastry on a floured surface to a rectangle about 14 × 18 inches. Trim the edges, removing a reasonably wide strip with a knife or pastry cutter to use as decoration later. Set aside.

Spread about one-third of the vegetable mixture in the middle of the pastry rectangle and place the meat on top. Distribute the rest of the vegetable mixture over the meat so that it is covered on all sides. Press it onto the meat firmly with your hand so that it does not fall off later. Fold one of the longer sides of the pastry rectangle over the meat and brush with beaten egg yolk. Bring up the opposite side of the pastry rectangle and press firmly onto the first layer of pastry. Brush the top with beaten egg yolk. Flatten the two ends a little, fold them over the top and press on firmly. Brush all the edges with beaten egg yolk and make sure that they are firmly sealed.

Dampen a baking sheet with cold water. Place the pastry-wrapped meat on the baking sheet, seam and folds underneath. Brush with beaten egg yolk and arrange half the reserved pastry strips diagonally on top as a decoration. Brush with egg yolk again and arrange the remaining strips on top in a criss-cross pattern. Brush with beaten egg yolk for the last time and set aside in a cool place for 15 minutes.

Preheat the oven to 400°F. Place the baking sheet in the heated oven and bake for 40 minutes. Open the oven door wide, switch off the oven and pull the beef close to the oven door. Let it rest in this position for about 10 minutes before serving.

1 **Covering the meat with the mixture.** Spread one-third of the mixture in the middle of the pastry rectangle and place the meat on top. Cover the meat with the rest of the mixture.

2 **Folding the pastry case.** Fold the longer sides over the meat first, brushing well with beaten egg yolk, then fold over the ends. Press to be sure all edges are firmly sealed.

3 **Decorating the package.** Place the pastry "package," seam down, on the baking sheet, brush with beaten egg yolk and arrange the pastry strips on top in a criss-cross pattern.

Steak and Kidney Pie

Everybody enjoys British steak and kidney pie and this version with mushrooms and onions is especially tasty. Make sure that the puff pastry lid fits tightly to keep in the different flavors.

Serves 4

$\frac{3}{4}$ lb frozen puff pastry
2 veal kidneys,
each weighing $\frac{1}{2}$ lb
$\frac{1}{2}$ lb boneless sirloin steak
1 cup button mushrooms
juice $\frac{1}{2}$ lemon
1 large onion
small bunch fresh parsley
freshly ground black pepper
$1\frac{1}{2}$ tablespoons flour
2 tablespoons vegetable oil
2 tablespoons butter
1 cup hot beef broth
Worcestershire sauce
2 tablespoons dry sherry
salt
1 egg yolk

Thawing time: 30 minutes
Preparation time: 1 hour

Lay the frozen puff pastry on the work surface and leave it to thaw.

To prepare the kidneys, rinse them under cold running water, pat dry and halve lengthwise. Remove any skin and fat, and cut out the cores. Do this carefully so that the kidneys keep their shape. Using a very sharp knife, slice the kidney halves. Dry the slices on paper towels. Remove any fat or gristle from the beef and wipe it with a damp cloth. Cut into 1 inch cubes. Clean the mushrooms and cut into thin slices. Sprinkle them immediately with lemon juice to prevent discoloration. Peel and dice the onion. Rinse the parsley, shake dry and chop finely.

Place the steak and kidney in a bowl, season generously with pepper and sprinkle with the flour. Toss to coat the meat. Heat the oil and butter in a skillet and brown the meat, in batches, over a high heat. Add more oil and butter if necessary. Remove the meat from the pan with a slotted spoon and place it in a deep pie or baking dish.

Add the mushrooms and onion to the fat in the skillet and brown them lightly. Remove with a slotted spoon and place them on top of the meat in the dish. Sprinkle with the chopped parsley.

Pour the hot broth into the skillet and bring to a boil, stirring to loosen any meat sediments in the pan. Season the broth with a dash of Worcestershire sauce, the sherry, and salt and pepper to taste and pour it over the contents in the dish.

Preheat the oven to 425°F. Roll out the puff pastry on a floured surface into a rectangle 2–2$\frac{1}{2}$ inches larger than the diameter of the pie dish. Cut a strip $\frac{3}{4}$ inch wide from the two long sides of the pastry rectangle. Dust the rolling pin with flour and wrap the rest of the pastry loosely around it. Brush the rim of the dish with cold water and place the strips of pastry on it. Press the ends of the pastry strips lightly together. Unroll the large piece of pastry over the dish and press on firmly at the edges. Cut off any excess pastry with a sharp knife or kitchen scissors. Holding a fork diagonally to the rim of the dish, press the pastry lid onto the strip so that the two are sealed together. Small pastry decorations for the lid can be made from the leftover pastry.

Prepare the lid by first cutting a hole in the middle, then brushing with beaten egg yolk and arranging the pastry decorations on top. Egg yolk holds the edges of pastry down so if you wish the decorations to rise properly, brush only the tops with egg yolk but not the edges.

Place the pie in the heated oven. Bake for 20 minutes, then reduce the temperature to 350°F and bake for a further 20 minutes. Cover the pastry with foil if it becomes too brown. Serve hot.

Our tip

For this recipe you will need a $1\frac{1}{2}$ quart capacity deep pie or baking dish with a wide unglazed rim. This will hold the pastry and prevent it from slipping into the pie filling.

1 **Putting on the pastry strips.** Brush the rim of the dish with cold water. Place the strips of puff pastry on the rim and press the ends together lightly.

2 **Putting on the pastry lid.** Use the rolling pin to lay the pastry lid over the pie dish. Press the edges down firmly before trimming off the excess pastry.

3 **Sealing the edges.** Hold a fork diagonally to the rim of the dish and press the pastry lid firmly to the strip. This will ensure a tight-fitting lid.

4 **Preparing the pie for the oven.** Cut a hole in the center of the pastry lid, brush with beaten egg yolk and place any pastry decorations on top. Brush the tops with egg yolk.

97

Tournedos Filled with Pâté

Filet mignons filled with pâté and green peppercorns and served with a sauce made from fresh mushrooms and cream are a delicacy for a very special occasion.

8 filet mignons, each
weighing about 3 oz
¾ cup button mushrooms
1 shallot
small bunch fresh parsley
3 tablespoons butter
6 tablespoons dry white wine
salt
freshly ground black pepper
2 oz good quality liver pâté
1 teaspoon green peppercorns
4 thin slices salt pork or bacon
2 tablespoons vegetable oil
2 tablespoons brandy
6 tablespoons heavy cream

Preparation time: 30 minutes

Press the steaks gently into a neat round shape using the ball of the thumb. Clean the mushrooms and chop finely. Peel and finely chop the shallot. Rinse the parsley, shake it dry and chop very finely.

Melt 1 tablespoon of the butter in a small pan and fry the shallot gently until it is soft. Add the mushrooms and fry, stirring all the time, until any juices have evaporated. Stir in the parsley and 2 tablespoons of the wine, and season to taste with salt and pepper. Cook until the liquid has evaporated. Remove from the heat and put aside to cool.

Mash the liver pâté and mix it with the drained green peppercorns and 2 table-spoons of the mushroom mixture. Divide the mixture among four of the steaks, spreading it evenly over the surface with a spoon or knife. Place the four remaining steaks on top of the filling and press together lightly. Wrap a slice of fatback or bacon around the sandwiched steaks and tie firmly with string. Cut the string just behind the knot.

Heat the oil with 1 tablespoon of the remaining butter in a skillet and sauté the steaks for 2–3 minutes on each side. Remove the steaks from the pan and keep warm. Pour the fat in which they were

sautéed and melt the rest of the butter in the skillet. Add the remaining mushroom mixture and heat through. Stir in the brandy and the remaining wine. Bring to a boil, then stir in the cream. Simmer, stirring constantly, until reduced to a creamy consistency. Season to taste with salt and pepper.

Remove the string from the steaks and place on a heated serving platter with or without the fat or bacon. Pour the sauce around them and serve immediately. Potato straws or sautéed potatoes and green beans or spinach with butter go well with this dish.

1 **Filling the steaks.** Divide the liver pâté mixture among the four steaks, spread evenly with a spoon or knife and place the remaining steaks on top. Press together lightly.

2 **Barding the steaks.** Wrap the slices of salt pork or bacon around the steaks, press it into place and tie securely with string. Cut the string just behind the knot.

3 **Preparing the sauce.** As soon as the mushroom and wine mixture is boiling fiercely, stir in the cream. Boil down, stirring all the time, until reduced to a creamy consistency.

Our tip

If you wish to make this fine dish even finer, use pâté de foie gras, and add a finely chopped truffle to it. If you prefer a more rustic flavor, prepare it as described in the recipe but add a little crushed garlic and chopped fresh marjoram or sage to the mushrooms during the first stage of cooking.

Boeuf à la Mode

It is worth taking the time to try this delicious French recipe.

Serves 6

½ lb salt pork
2 small bay leaves
pinch dried thyme
salt
freshly ground black pepper
¼ cup brandy
1 bunch fresh parsley
3–4 cloves garlic
1 boneless beef rump roast,
weighing about 2 lb
1½ cups
full-bodied dry white wine
2 onions
2 carrots
2 calf's or pig's feet
2 oz fresh pork skin
(if available)
2 tablespoons lard
1½–2 cups beef broth
¾ lb small early carrots
6 oz small onions
2 tablespoons butter

To marinate and cool: 5¼ hours
Preparation time: 3–3½ hours

Cut the salt pork into strips as long and as thin as pencils and put them on a plate. Grind half a bay leaf with a pinch of thyme in a mortar with a pestle and mix with some salt and pepper. Sprinkle the seasoning mixture over the pork strips (called lardoons), then pour over 1½ tablespoons of the brandy. Cover with a plate and chill for 30 minutes.

Rinse the parsley and shake dry. Finely chop one-quarter of the parsley, and set aside the remainder. Peel and very finely chop one clove of garlic. Mix the parsley with the garlic, sprinkle over the lardoons and turn to coat them. In this way they acquire an aroma which will seep through the meat later during cooking.

To prepare the meat for larding, use a thin sharpening steel to penetrate right through the meat parallel to the grain. Thread the lardoons into a larding needle and pull them through the holes made by the sharpening steel. Tie the meat into a neat shape if necessary and place in a deep bowl that is only slightly larger than the meat itself. Pour the wine and the remaining brandy over the meat and add the remaining bay leaves. Peel the 2 onions, 2 carrots and the remaining cloves of garlic and chop coarsely. Place around the meat in the bowl. Cover the bowl and put it in a cool place (not the refrigerator) for 5 hours to marinate. Turn the meat frequently.

Preheat the oven to 300°F. Rinse the calf's or pig's feet and pork skin. Place them in a saucepan, cover with cold water and bring to a boil. Boil for 5 minutes, then drain and rinse under cold water. Chop into pieces.

Heat the lard in a large flameproof casserole. Remove the meat from the marinade and dry well with paper towels. Place in the hot fat and brown well on all sides. Remove the chopped carrots, onions and garlic from the bowl, drain well and place in the fat. Fry, turning, until golden. Add the pieces of calf's or pig's feet, the pork skin and the rest of the parsley. Season to taste with salt, pepper and thyme. Strain the marinade from the bowl into the casserole. Add enough broth to cover the meat. Cover the casserole tightly and place in the heated oven. Cook for 2½–3 hours.

Thirty minutes before the end of the cooking time, prepare the early carrots and small onions. Scrape the carrots, and peel the onions. Melt the butter in a skillet and turn the vegetables in it until they begin to take on color. Add a very little broth to prevent them from burning and cook over a gentle heat until tender. Season to taste with salt and pepper.

Remove the meat from the casserole and keep warm. Strain the stock and skim off all the fat. Return to the casserole and boil the stock to reduce it a little. Slice the meat and arrange it on a heated serving platter with the early carrots and onions all around. Pour a little of the stock over the vegetables and serve the rest separately.

1 Seasoning the lardoons. Sprinkle the lardoons with the mixture of bay leaf, thyme, salt and pepper, and pour the brandy over them. Cover and chill for 30 minutes.

2 Preparing the meat for larding. Turn the lardoons in the mixture of parsley and garlic. Pierce right through the meat parallel to the grain with a thin sharpening steel.

3 Larding the meat. Pull the seasoned lardoons through the meat with a larding needle. Tie the meat into a neat shape if necessary, then marinate.

4 Straining the marinade. As soon as the meat and vegetables are well colored, strain the marinade through a sieve into the casserole. Add enough broth to cover the meat.

Our tip

Ask your butcher to cut you a roast that you can lard parallel to the grain of the meat. The meat from the calf's or pig's feet and the pork skin can be served with the meat, if desired.

Traditional Roast Beef

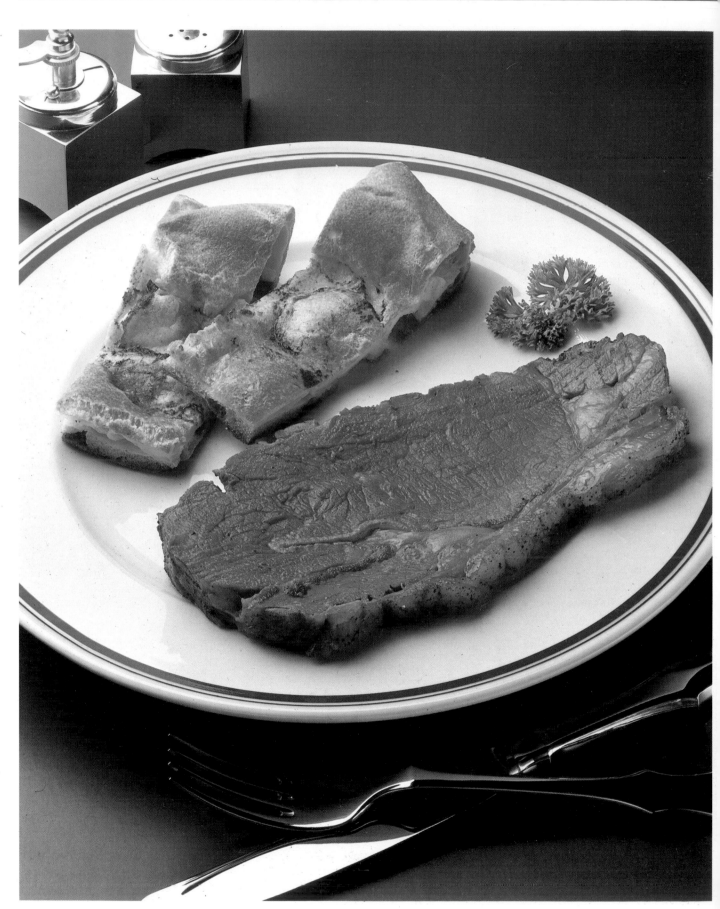

Large cuts of tender beef, such as rib, tenderloin or sirloin tip, are all suitable for roasting. The roast should be moist and juicy, never overcooked or dry, and Yorkshire pudding, roast potatoes, horseradish sauce and gravy made from the pan juices are excellent accompaniments.

Whether the beef is rare, medium or well done depends on personal taste and the cooking time should be calculated according to the times given below. Allow 15 minutes per pound if you want a rare roast, 20 minutes per pound for a medium roast or 25 minutes per pound for a well-done roast. A meat theremometer can also be used as a guide. Insert the thermometer into the thickest part of the roast before cooking, then check the temperature when you think the meat should be cooked. A reading of 140°F indicates that the meat is rare, 160°F means that the meat is medium and 170°F gives a well-done roast.

Place the meat in the roasting pan, fat side uppermost. If preferred, the excess fat from a rolled rib roast may be trimmed off before cooking. Rub the fat with salt and dot with beef drippings. If roast potatoes are cooked with the meat, they should be cut into even-sized pieces, blanched in boiling salted water for 2–3 minutes, then arranged around the meat in the pan. Roast in a preheated 425–450°F oven for the first 15 minutes to seal the outside of the roast. Reduce the oven temperature to 350–375°F and con-

tinue cooking until done to taste. Baste the meat and potatoes frequently during cooking to prevent the surface from drying out.

Traditionally, roasting is a method of cooking meat on a rack above a pan so that the fat runs off the meat. The fat has to be scored to allow the drippings to run freely and keep the meat moist during cooking. The Yorkshire pudding is then cooked in the pan below the meat for the last 40–45 minutes of roasting time.

For the Yorkshire pudding, sift 1 cup flour into a bowl with $\frac{1}{8}$ teaspoon of salt. Make a well in the middle of the flour and add 2 eggs with a little milk taken from $1\frac{1}{2}$ cups. Whisk or beat the eggs and milk together, gradually working in the flour from the sides and adding the remaining milk. Whisk or beat the batter until it is quite smooth, then stir in 2 tablespoons water and allow to stand for about 15 minutes.

Pour off most of the fat from the pan below the meat – reserve this for the gravy – or, remove a little of the fat from around the meat and pour it into a separate roasting pan. Return the pan to the oven until the fat is hot, then pour in the batter and cook with the meat for about 40–45 minutes.

To make gravy to accompany the meat, pour off most of the fat from the roasting pan, leaving just a thin covering in the bottom of the pan. Over low heat, and stirring continuously, add 1–3 tablespoons flour to the pan. Cook, stirring the juices out of the corners, for a few

minutes, then gradually pour in about 2 cups beef broth or vegetable cooking liquid. Bring to a boil, stirring continuously, and simmer for a few minutes. Stir up the juices from the bottom of the pan to flavor the gravy.

Serve the meat on a large platter, surrounded by the potatoes and accompanied by the Yorkshire pudding. Pour the gravy into a warmed sauce boat and serve separately.

1 Score the fat for traditional roasting. Use a sharp knife and cut a criss-cross pattern in the fat. This will allow the drippings to run freely, and keep the meat moist during cooking.

2 Preparing the Yorkshire pudding. Sift the flour into a bowl, make a well in the center and add the eggs. Mix to a smooth batter with the milk, using an electric beater.

3 Roasting the meat. Place the pudding batter in the pan under the meat, so that it will catch all the juices and cook for 40–45 minutes or until golden and puffed up.

Beef Stroganoff

Elegant dishes are not necessarily difficult to prepare. Beef stroganoff is a good example. It is quick and easy to prepare and should be brought to the table as quickly as possible when ready.

1½ lb boneless sirloin steak
2 onions
5 tablespoons butter
5 tablespoons hot beef broth
1 tablespoon tomato paste
½ teaspoon prepared mustard
1 cup sour cream
salt
freshly ground black pepper
wine vinegar or lemon juice

Preparation time: 30 minutes

Carefully remove any fat or gristle from the steak. Cut the meat into slices ½ inch wide and the slices into strips ½ inch wide. The meat should on no account be cut too thin or it may become hard and tough while cooking. Peel the onions and chop finely.

Melt about 2 tablespoons of the butter in a large heavy skillet. Add a portion of the meat strips and brown on all sides over a moderate heat, stirring all the time. Remove the meat and place it in a sieve with a plate underneath to catch any meat juices. Continue frying the meat in portions, adding more butter to the pan as necessary. When all the meat has been browned, add the onions to the pan and fry until soft and golden. Pour in the hot broth and bring to a boil, stirring to loosen any meat sediments on the bottom and sides of the pan.

Add the tomato paste, mustard and sour cream and mix everything together well, stirring constantly. Season to taste with salt, pepper and a dash of wine vinegar or lemon juice. Add the meat strips with any meat juices which have dripped onto the plate. Quickly heat the meat through again, but do not let the sauce boil or the meat will become hard and tough and the sour cream may separate. Place on a heated serving dish and serve immediately.

A selection of vegetables cooked in butter (for example, peas, early carrots, mushrooms or asparagus) or a plain green salad with boiled potatoes or rice go well with this dish.

1 **Cutting the steak into strips.** First trim any fat or gristle from the meat. Cut into slices $\frac{1}{2}$ inch wide and the slices into strips $\frac{1}{2}$ inch wide. Do not slice too thinly.

2 **Stirring in the sour cream.** As soon as the onion is soft and golden, add the broth followed by the tomato paste, mustard and sour cream. Season to taste with salt, pepper and vinegar or lemon juice.

3 **Adding the steak strips.** Place the steak strips and the meat juices in the sauce and mix together. Heat through once more, but do not allow to boil or the sour cream may separate.

Our tip

The classic recipe for beef stroganoff has been argued about for a long time. The experts agree only on three ingredients: steak, onions and sour cream. However, there are many variations. Some cooks add a few thinly sliced mushrooms to the onions, others add tiny strips of gherkin and/or season with a little paprika. There are also those who add potato or beet slices.

Paupiettes of Beef

These paupiettes of beef contain interesting new fillings: on the left, zucchini and tomato; in the middle, beef and tongue; and on the right, egg and spinach. The preparation remains basically the same.

Serves 4

*For the zucchini and
tomato filling:*
1 large ripe tomato
2 cloves garlic
1 bunch fresh basil
2 sprigs fresh oregano
1 teaspoon olive oil
salt
freshly ground black pepper
4 very small zucchini
2 oz goat's milk or
other soft, crumbly cheese

4 thin slices beef top round
steak, each weighing $\frac{1}{2}$ lb
1 onion
1 sprig fresh parsley
1 stalk celery
1 leek
2 tablespoons vegetable oil
2 tablespoons butter
2 cups hot beef broth
1 bay leaf
$\frac{3}{4}$ cup sour cream

Preparation time: $1\frac{1}{2}$–2 hours

To make the filling, scald the tomato in boiling water for 10 seconds, then peel and remove the core and any pieces of hard stem. Cut in half so that all seed chambers are visible and, taking half a tomato at a time in the palm of your hand, squeeze gently until the seeds fall out, then discard them. Chop the tomato finely. Peel and crush the garlic. Rinse the herbs, shake them dry and chop finely. Heat the oil in a small pan and fry the tomato and garlic until it is a smooth purée. Season to taste with salt and pepper, stir in the chopped herbs and set aside to cool. Rinse the zucchini, dry well and trim off the ends. Crumble the cheese.

Pat the beef slices dry and season with salt and pepper. Spread the tomato and garlic purée evenly over each slice of beef and sprinkle with the cheese. Place one zucchini on each slice and roll up tightly. Fasten the paupiettes by inserting wooden toothpicks or metal skewers through the two upper layers of meat, or tie them up with thread.

Peel the onion. Rinse the parsley and shake dry. Trim the celery and leek. Chop everything coarsely.

Heat the oil and butter in a large heavy skillet and brown the paupiettes well on all sides. Add the prepared vegetables and continue frying until they are golden brown. Add a little of the hot broth and stir well to loosen any meat sediment on the bottom of the pan. Let the broth boil down before adding the remaining broth. Season to taste with salt and pepper and add the bay leaf and chopped parsley. Reduce the heat and simmer gently for 1–$1\frac{1}{4}$ hours or until the paupiettes are tender.

Remove the paupiettes from the pan and keep warm. Strain the stock and return to the pan. Boil down until well reduced, then stir in the sour cream and heat through gently. Remove the toothpicks or thread and serve the paupiettes with the sauce.

Beet and tongue filling: Season the beef slices and spread with prepared mustard. Mix together $\frac{1}{2}$ lb cooked tongue, chopped, 1 small cooked beet, peeled and chopped, 1 apple, peeled, cored and chopped, and 1 onion, peeled and chopped. Spread over the mustard on the beef slices. Rinse and shake dry a few sprigs of fresh dill and chop finely. Sprinkle on top, then roll up the beef slices tightly. Proceed as described in the basic recipe.

Spinach and egg filling: Prepare $\frac{1}{2}$ lb fresh spinach and blanch it in boiling water for 3 minutes. Drain and plunge into ice cold water, then drain again. Peel and finely chop 1 onion and 1 clove of garlic and fry in 1 teaspoon olive oil until soft. Place the drained spinach in the pan and cook for a few minutes with the onion and garlic. Put aside to cool. When the filling has cooled, season to taste with salt, pepper and grated nutmeg and mix in $\frac{1}{4}$ cup grated Parmesan cheese and $\frac{1}{3}$ cup grated

Swiss cheese. Divide the filling between the four slices of beef and place one shelled, hard-cooked egg on each slice. Roll up tightly and proceed as described in the basic recipe.

You can use small metal skewers to fasten the paupiettes, or wooden toothpicks, or you can tie them into shape with thread or butcher's string. It is also possible to obtain special clips in some stores. Whatever is used, remember to remove it before serving the paupiettes.

1 **Filling the paupiettes.** Season the beef slices with salt and pepper. Spread the tomato and garlic purée over the meat and sprinkle with the crumbled cheese.

2 **Rolling up the beef.** Place a small zucchini across a slice of beef at one end, fold the end over it and roll up tightly. Repeat with the remaining slices.

3 **Fastening the paupiettes.** Fasten each paupiette with a small skewer or wooden toothpick, which should be pushed through the two upper layers of meat.

4 **Adding the broth.** When the vegetables are golden brown, add a little hot broth and stir to loosen any meat sediments on the bottom of the pan. Boil down, then add the remainder.

Stuffed Pork

Stuffed pork is just the right thing for those who enjoy a hearty meal. And this is an economical dish, too. A refreshing glass of beer makes a suitable liquid accompaniment.

1 boned fresh
picnic pork roast,
weighing 2 lb
salt
freshly ground black pepper
1 tablespoon prepared mustard
2 leeks
1 stale roll
$\frac{1}{4}$ cup hot milk
2 egg yolks
$\frac{1}{2}$ small sweet red pepper
$\frac{3}{4}$ cup canned
whole kernel corn
2 cups hot beef broth
2 onions
1 carrot
1 stalk celery
small bunch fresh parsley
1 large ripe tomato

Preparation time: 2$\frac{1}{4}$ hours

Ask your butcher to cut a pocket in the meat which should almost go through to the other side. Pat the meat dry inside and out. Season with salt and pepper and spread the inside of the pocket with the mustard. If the rind is on the meat, take a very sharp knife and score a criss-cross pattern in the rind without damaging the meat underneath. (If you prefer, this can be done after stuffing the meat.)

Preheat the oven to 425°F. Prepare the leeks by trimming off the dark green leaves and the roots. Cut halfway into the upper, white part of the leeks lengthwise, taking care not to cut the leeks in half. Rinse thoroughly under cold running water to remove any dirt hidden between the leaves, and drain well. Blanch in boiling salted water for 3 minutes, then plunge into cold water. Drain and put aside to cool.

Chop the roll into pieces and place in a bowl with the hot milk. Leave to soften for 10 minutes, then squeeze out the excess milk. Place the bread in a bowl with the beaten egg yolks. Remove the core and seeds from the red pepper, and cut into $\frac{1}{4}$ inch dice. Add to the bowl with the drained corn. Mix everything together thoroughly and season to taste with salt and pepper.

Press the corn mixture firmly into the pocket in the meat, then push in the two leeks so that they are both surrounded by the corn mixture. Sew up the pocket and place the meat, with the rind at the bottom, in a roasting pan. Pour over half the broth and place in the heated oven. Cook for 15 minutes.

Meanwhile, peel the onions and carrot. Trim the celery. Rinse the parsley and shake dry. Chop everything coarsely. Rinse the tomato, cut out the core and chop it coarsely.

Remove the roasting pan from the oven and turn the meat so that the rind is at the top. Arrange the chopped vegetables and parsley around the meat and return to the oven. Reduce the heat to 375°F. Cook for a further 1$\frac{1}{2}$ hours, adding a little more broth from time to time so that the vegetables do not burn.

When the meat is ready, remove it from the pan and keep warm. Add the rest of the broth to the pan and stir well to loosen any meat sediments on the bottom. Bring to a boil, stirring. Skim off as much fat as possible, then strain the liquid through a sieve into a saucepan, pressing the vegetables through the fine mesh of the sieve with a spoon. Thicken the gravy by boiling it down. Season to taste with salt and pepper. After removing the thread, slice the meat and serve with the gravy.

1 Preparing the leeks. Remove the coarse dark green leaves and the roots, then cut open the upper half of the stem lengthwise without cutting right through the leek. Rinse thoroughly.

2 Stuffing the pork. Fill the pocket with the corn mixture and push in the leeks through so that they are completely surrounded by the corn stuffing.

3 Preparing the gravy. Loosen any meat sediments by boiling the rest of the broth in the roasting pan. Skim off the fat and strain the liquid. Pass the vegetables through the sieve.

Roast Pork Danish Style

This roast, slowly cooked in wine and cream, is enhanced by a filling of sweet prunes, tart apples and aromatic herbs. It is a dish for those who appreciate hearty home cooking.

Serves 6

½ cup prunes
1 boneless pork loin,
weighing 1¾–2 lb
salt
freshly ground black pepper
1 small tart apple · juice ½ lemon
2 sprigs fresh or
½ teaspoon dried marjoram
2 sprigs fresh or
½ teaspoon dried thyme
2 tablespoons oil
2 tablespoons butter
6 tablespoons full-bodied
dry white wine
1¼ cups light cream
1–2 tablespoons currant jelly

Soaking time (prunes): 30 minutes
Preparation time: 1¾ hours

Soak the prunes in hot water for 30 minutes. Meanwhile, score a cross in each end of the meat, then push a sharpening steel lengthwise through the meat to make room for the filling. Season the opening with salt and pepper.

Peel, core and finely chop the apple. Sprinkle with the lemon juice to prevent discoloration. Rinse the herbs, shake dry and chop half of them. Drain the prunes and pit them. Mix the prunes with the apples and herbs and stuff this filling into the pork, using the handle of a wooden spoon to press it through.

Take a long piece of string and make a loop at one end. Pull the loop tightly around one end of the meat, pulling the other end of the string through and binding it around again and again. Secure it at the top so that the roast has the shape of a long narrow bolster. Season with salt and pepper. Preheat the oven to 350°F.

Heat the oil and butter in a roasting pan on top of the range and sear the meat well on all sides. This should take about 20 minutes. Remove the meat and care-fully pour off any excess fat from the pan. Return the pan to the heat and pour in the wine, then add the cream, stirring vigorously all the time. Return the meat to the pan. Heat the liquid almost to boiling point. Season to taste with salt and pepper and add the rest of the herbs. Cover the pan and place in the heated oven. Roast for 1 hour.

Remove the meat from the pan when it is cooked and keep warm. Skim off any fat from the liquid and strain into a saucepan. Stir in the currant jelly and boil down over a strong heat until the sauce becomes creamy in consistency. Taste and adjust the seasoning.

Remove the string from the meat and cut into slices ½ inch thick. Serve the slices on a heated platter with a little of the sauce separately. Boiled potatoes, braised red cabbage or even a green salad go well with this dish. A dry white wine makes a good accompanying drink.

Our tip

You will find it even easier to stuff the pork if you cut a pocket in the meat. Begin about $\frac{3}{4}$ inch away from one end of the roast and cut a clean, deep slit, running the whole length of the roast, stopping well short of cutting all the way through to the bottom. Leave another $\frac{3}{4}$ inch uncut at the opposite end of the meat as well so that the stuffing cannot fall out during cooking or turning the meat. Season the inside of the meat, fill it with the apple mixture and sew the opening tightly together again. Before carving and serving the meat you will of course have to remove all the threads.

1 **Preparing the pork.** Score a cross in each end of the meat, then push a sharpening steel through the meat to make a tunnel for the filling. Season the opening with salt and pepper.

2 **Stuffing the meat.** Push the apple, prune and herb mixture into the tunnel in the loin of pork and press it through with the handle of a wooden spoon.

3 **Tying the meat.** Tie string around the meat, looping it as a butcher does. Secure it at the top and finish with a firm knot. Season the meat with salt and pepper.

Pork Tenderloin with Peas

Pork tenderloin with peas is a dish which has its origins in the Far East. Serve it Asian style, with a bowl of rice.

Serves 4

1 lb pork tenderloin
1 egg white
1 tablespoon cornstarch
3 tablespoons soy sauce
4–5 tablespoons rice wine
or dry sherry
freshly ground black pepper
1 cup frozen peas
salt
1 leek
1 shallot
1 clove garlic
1 cup canned bamboo shoots
2 tablespoons sesame seeds
$\frac{1}{4}$ cup peanut oil
1 teaspoon green peppercorns
6 tablespoons hot chicken broth
pinch ground ginger (optional)

To marinate: 40 minutes
Preparation time: 30 minutes

Wipe the pork with a damp cloth and pat dry. Cut the meat into slices $\frac{1}{4}$ inch thick, cutting across or diagonally to the grain of the meat (this will depend on the thickness of the tenderloin). Halve the slices lengthwise. Mix the egg white and cornstarch together in a bowl. Add half the soy sauce, about 3 tablespoons of the rice wine or dry sherry and a little freshly ground black pepper. Beat the ingredients together vigorously. Place the meat strips in the marinade, cover the bowl and leave in a cool place (not the refrigerator) for 40 minutes.

Meanwhile, cook the peas in boiling salted water as directed on the package. Drain in a sieve, then rinse under cold running water to cool. Drain again and set aside. Trim the roots and dark green leaves from the leek. Cut into pieces $1\frac{1}{2}$ inches long, then cut these lengthwise into strips $\frac{1}{8}$ inch wide. Place the strips in a sieve under cold running water and rinse thoroughly to remove any grit that might remain. Put aside to drain. Peel the shallot and garlic. Dice the shallot and chop the garlic very finely. Drain the bamboo shoots and cut them into strips $\frac{1}{8}$ inch wide.

When the meat has been in the marinade for 40 minutes, heat a wok or skillet. When the pan is really hot, place the sesame seeds in it and toast them until they are golden in color, stirring all the time so that they do not burn. Remove from the pan and set aside.

Heat a little of the oil in the pan. Add the meat strips, a few at a time, and fry briskly until browned on all sides. Remove from the pan and place in a sieve with a plate underneath to catch the meat juices. Add a little more oil to the pan when necessary. When all the meat has been browned, place the leek, shallot, garlic and bamboo shoots in the pan and stir-fry until they are glassy in appearance. Stir in the peas, green peppercorns and hot chicken broth and bring to a boil. Boil briskly for 1–2 minutes, or until the vegetables are just tender.

Return the meat to the pan, with any meat juices. Warm everything through again but do not boil. Add the rest of the soy sauce and rice wine or sherry, and season to taste with a little salt and/or ground ginger. Serve immediately, sprinkled with the sesame seeds, so that the vegetables lose nothing of their crisp freshness.

1 **Marinating the meat.** Place the strips of pork tenderloin in the marinade, cover and leave in a cool place for 40 minutes. Meanwhile, cook the peas as directed on the package.

2 **Chopping the leek.** First cut the leek into 1½ inch lengths and then into strips ⅛ inch wide. Place in a sieve and rinse thoroughly under cold running water.

3 **Toasting the sesame seeds.** Place the seeds in a hot wok or frying pan, without fat. Toast them over a high heat, stirring constantly, until they are golden.

4 **Adding the meat.** As soon as the vegetables are just tender, return the pork to the pan with any meat juices. Heat through, but do not allow to boil.

Our tip

It is important to cook the pork quickly so that it remains tender. Fry small portions at a time and stir constantly so that the pork is seared on all sides as quickly as possible. Meat that begins to cook in its own juices easily becomes tough.

Marinated Leg of Lamb

Roast leg of lamb should be moist and juicy in the middle and is at its best when rare, as shown in the photograph.

4–6 cloves garlic
freshly ground black pepper
1–2 tablespoons Armagnac or Cognac
3 tablespoons olive oil
3 sprigs fresh or
½ teaspoon dried rosemary
small bunch fresh or
1 teaspoon dried thyme
2 bay leaves
1 French-style leg of lamb,
weighing about 2 lb
¼ cup butter, softened
salt

To marinate: 12–24 hours
Preparation time: 1¼ hours

Peel the cloves of garlic and chop very finely or crush in a garlic press. Sprinkle with freshly ground black pepper (about ½ teaspoon) and mix with the Armagnac or Cognac. Beat in the oil, drop by drop. Rinse the rosemary and thyme and shake dry. Strip the needle-like leaves from the rosemary and chop the thyme roughly. Spread a large piece of extra strong aluminum foil on the work surface and sprinkle a little of the rosemary and thyme in the middle. Crumble one of the bay leaves over the herbs.

Wipe the lamb with a damp cloth and pat dry with paper towels. Brush the meat with the garlic and oil mixture and put it on top of the herbs on the foil. Sprinkle the remaining herbs over the meat and wrap it tightly in foil so that none of the aroma of the seasonings can be lost. Place the lamb in a cool place and leave to marinate overnight or, even better, for 24 hours; a cool pantry is better than the refrigerator. If you do not have a cool pantry, the refrigerator can be used but the meat should be removed 2 hours before cooking time since the aroma can develop better in the foil at room temperature.

When you are ready to cook the lamb preheat the oven to 475°F. Unwrap the meat and carefully scrape off the herb and garlic mixture or wipe it off with paper towels. This is very important for if it is not completely removed, it will burn during cooking and taste bitter. Pat the lamb dry with paper towels. Brush two-thirds of the softened butter evenly over the meat, then season it on all sides with salt. If you are using a meat thermometer, insert it into the thickest part of the meat, making sure that the needle does not touch the bone.

Place the meat on an oven shelf over a roasting pan, or on a rack in a pan, in the heated oven. Reduce the temperature to 400°F and roast the meat for 45 minutes to 1 hour, or until the meat thermometer registers 160°F for medium rare or 175°F for well done. Baste frequently with the remaining butter during this time.

Remove the meat from the oven and let it rest, loosely wrapped in foil, for 10–15 minutes. Slice the meat on a slant to the bone or grain of the meat and season again with salt and pepper if desired. Serve hot.

1 **Marinating the lamb.** Brush the meat all over with the garlic and oil mixture and place on top of the herbs on the foil. Distribute the remaining herbs over the meat and wrap tightly in foil.

2 **Brushing the meat with butter.** Scrape off the herbs and garlic mixture, then spread two-thirds of the softened butter over the meat. Season with salt. Reserve the rest of the butter for basting.

3 **Inserting the meat thermometer.** If you are using a meat thermometer, insert it into the thickest part of the meat. The needle should not touch the bone. Place the meat on an oven shelf over a roasting pan or on a roasting rack in a pan.

Crown Roast of Lamb with Green Beans

A crown roast of lamb is not difficult to make and is always appropriate for an elegant dinner party.

Serves 8

2 racks of lamb, each
weighing 2–2½ lb
1 sprig fresh or
¼ teaspoon dried rosemary
2 sprigs fresh or
½ teaspoon dried thyme
3–4 cloves garlic
pinch dried sage
¼ cup olive oil · salt
freshly ground black pepper
2 tablespoons butter
1 onion · 1 carrot
1 stalk celery
1 bunch fresh parsley
6 tablespoons full-bodied
dry red wine
6 tablespoons hot beef broth
6 tablespoons heavy cream

For the garnish:
1 lb tender young green beans
salt · 1 onion
2 cloves garlic
2 large ripe tomatoes
1 bunch fresh or
1 teaspoon dried basil
1 sprig fresh or
¼ teaspoon dried thyme
2 tablespoons olive oil

To marinate: 18–24 hours
Preparation time: 2 hours

Carefully remove any pieces of skin or sinew from the meat and trim back any thick layers of fat. Remove any small bone splinters with a damp cloth. Trim the ends of the bones by cutting off about 1½ inches of skin and the thin layer of meat which lies directly on the bone. Place the meat fat side down on the work surface.

In order to stretch the racks to make the crown, it is necessary to cut into the meat between every second rib chop and pull the bones apart a little towards the inside while this is being done so that it is easier to shape and bind later. Form the crown by bending the racks around with the fat facing the inside until the ends

meet. Secure by inserting wooden toothpicks through the upper part of the meat. Once the crown has been formed and pinned together, it can be tied with string. Draw the string around the lower part of the crown, pull it tight and tie with a firm knot.

Rinse the rosemary and thyme, pat them dry and chop. Peel 2–3 cloves of garlic and chop them finely or crush with a little salt in a garlic press. Mix the garlic, rosemary, thyme, sage and 2 tablespoons of the oil to a paste. Rub the mixture over the crown then wrap it in aluminum foil and set aside to marinate for 18–24 hours.

About 1 hour before the lamb is to be served, preheat the oven to 450°F. Unwrap the crown and scrape off the herb mixture. Season the meat with salt and pepper and brush it all over with 1 tablespoon of the remaining oil. Heat the rest of the oil and the butter in a flat roasting pan. Place the meat in the fat and put the pan in the heated oven. Roast for 15 minutes.

Meanwhile, peel the remaining garlic, the onion and carrot. Trim the celery. Chop everything coarsely. Rinse the parsley, shake it dry and chop. When the meat has been in the oven for 15 minutes, place the vegetables and herbs in the roasting pan around the roast and let them go nicely brown in the hot fat. Continue roasting for about 30 minutes. Mix the wine and broth together and add just enough liquid to the pan from time to time to prevent the herbs and vegetables from burning.

Remove the roast when it is ready and wrap it loosely in foil. Put it to rest in a warm place for 15 minutes. Pour the rest of the wine and broth mixture into the pan and bring to a boil on top of the range, stirring to loosen any meat sediments. Strain the liquid into a saucepan. Stir in the cream and boil rapidly to reduce to a creamy gravy. Keep warm.

To prepare the beans, trim, and break into pieces about 1½ inches in length. Cook in boiling salted water for 8 minutes. Place in a sieve and rinse under cold water to cool. Put aside to drain.

Peel the onion and slice into rings. Peel and crush the garlic. Scald the tomatoes in boiling water for 10 seconds, then peel and remove the core and any pieces of hard stem. Cut in half so that all seed

chambers are visible and, taking half a tomato at a time in the palm of your hand, squeeze gently until the seeds fall out. Discard the seeds. Chop the tomatoes coarsely. Rinse the herbs, shake dry and chop.

Heat the oil in a skillet and fry the onions and garlic until they are soft and golden. Add the beans and heat them through. Stir in the tomatoes, and season to taste with salt and pepper. Add the herbs and mix well.

Place the crown roast of lamb on a heated serving platter and remove the string. Arrange the beans in the middle and around the edges of the crown. Serve very hot, with the gravy.

1 **Stretching the racks.** Cut a little way into the meat between every second bone and pull the bones away from one another slightly, bending the meat towards the inside.

2 **Shaping the crown.** Bend the racks around with the fat to the inside until the ends meet. Secure with wooden toothpicks through the upper part of the meat.

3 **Tying the roast.** Bind the string around the lower part of the crown, pull as tightly as possible and tie with a firm knot. The roast should now be marinated.

4 **Adding the wine and broth.** Mix the wine and broth together, and from time to time add just enough liquid to prevent the herbs and vegetables from burning.

Our tip

When the rib bones are trimmed, the skin and a little meat will be removed; this can be added to a soup or stew so that there is no waste.

Loin of Lamb with Herbs and Garlic

The spicy crust made of herbs and garlic gives the tender lamb an unusual fragrance. Serve with young green beans and sautéed potatoes.

Serves 6

1 whole bulb garlic
1 onion
6 tablespoons beef broth
1 sprig fresh or
$\frac{1}{4}$ teaspoon dried rosemary
2 sprigs fresh or
$\frac{1}{2}$ teaspoon dried thyme
1 bunch fresh parsley
salt
freshly ground black pepper
2 tablespoons Dijon-style mustard
$\frac{1}{2}$ cup soft bread crumbs
$\frac{1}{4}$ cup olive oil
1 lamb sirloin roast or
double loin roast,
weighing $2\frac{1}{2}$–3 lb

Preparation time: $1\frac{1}{2}$ hours

Bring a saucepan of water to a boil. Peel the cloves of garlic and drop into the boiling water. Bring to a boil again, then drain the garlic and plunge into ice-cold water. Drain again.

Peel the onion and chop coarsely. Place in a small saucepan with the garlic and cover with the broth. Bring to a boil, then simmer over a gentle heat for about 25 minutes or until the onion and garlic are soft.

Meanwhile, rinse the herbs, shake dry and strip the leaves from the stalks. Chop the leaves very finely and place in a bowl.

Put the garlic and onion in a blender or processor and reduce to a purée, or chop to a fine pulp. Put in the bowl with the herbs and season to taste with salt and pepper. Mix in the mustard and bread crumbs. Add a few drops of olive oil and stir until the mixture has a smooth consistency.

Preheat the oven to 425°F. Wipe the meat with a damp cloth and pat dry with paper towels. Season all over with salt and pepper, and score the fat in a criss-cross pattern with a sharp knife. Heat half the remaining olive oil in a large flame-proof casserole or flat roasting pan and brown the meat well on all sides over a high heat.

Spread the garlic and herb mixture evenly over the fat side of the lamb. Smooth it carefully with the back of a spoon. Sprinkle the rest of the oil over the mixture and place the roast in the heated oven. Cook for 30–40 minutes, or until the meat is cooked to your liking, and the herb crust is golden brown.

Remove the meat from the oven, cover loosely with a sheet of foil and allow to rest in a warm place for 10–15 minutes. Slice the meat lengthwise along the backbone and then in slices from the backbone towards the edges. Serve hot.

1 **Blanching the garlic.** Place the garlic cloves in the rapidly boiling water and let it return to a boil. Drain the garlic and plunge into ice cold water. Drain again.

2 **Making the garlic crust.** Mix the garlic and onion purée with the herbs, bread crumbs, mustard and a few drops of olive oil. Season to taste with salt and pepper and mix to a smooth paste.

3 **Coating the roast.** Spread the herb and garlic mixture on the fat side of the roast and smooth over carefully. Sprinkle with the rest of the oil and place the meat in the oven.

Oriental Lamb Pilaff

Oriental lamb pilaff is a fascinating and unusual mixture of savory lamb, fresh grapes and sweet raisins.

Serves 4

1 lb lean boneless lamb,
from the leg
2 onions
1 clove garlic
1 sweet red pepper
small bunch (about 5 oz)
seedless grapes
3 tablespoons raisins
5 tablespoons butter
salt
freshly ground black pepper
$\frac{1}{8}$ teaspoon ground ginger
2 cups hot beef broth
$\frac{3}{4}$ cup long-grain rice

Preparation time: 45 minutes

Cut the meat into $\frac{3}{4}$ inch cubes. Peel the onions and garlic. Chop the onions finely, and chop or crush the garlic. Halve the red pepper and remove the core and seeds. Rinse in cold water, drain and chop into $\frac{3}{4}$ inch squares. Rinse the grapes in warm water, pluck them from the stems and put them to drain in a sieve or colander. Rinse the raisins in hot water and place in the sieve with the grapes.

Heat 3 tablespoons of the butter in a large skillet and sear the meat cubes, a few at a time, on all sides over a strong heat. When all the meat has been browned, add the onions and garlic and fry, stirring frequently until they begin to color. Add the pieces of red pepper and fry them until they are soft. Do not let them brown. Return the meat cubes to the pan.

Place the drained grapes and raisins in the skillet. Season to taste with salt, pepper and ginger and mix everything together well, being careful not to crush the grapes. Pour the hot broth into the pan, bring to a boil and simmer over a gentle heat for 20–30 minutes.

Cook the rice according to the package directions. If using a short-grain or starchy rice, rinse the rice under cold water before cooking.

Dot the rice with the rest of the butter.

Mix it in with two forks until it has melted and combined with the rice. Put the rice into a ring mold, press it in lightly and then unmold onto a heated serving dish. Place the lamb mixture in the ring and serve immediately.

1 **Adding the fruit.** Place the drained grapes and raisins in the skillet, season with salt, pepper and ginger and mix everything together without crushing the grapes.

2 **Rinsing the rice.** Rinse the rice under cold running water until the water running out of the sieve is clear and therefore free of starch. Drain well, then cook in salted water.

3 **Mixing in the butter.** Dot the rest of the butter over the rice and mix it in with two forks until it has melted and all the grains of rice are coated. Press into a ring mold.

Our tip

The meat, rice and other ingredients can be cooked together as in a risotto, if preferred. In that case, remove the meat from the pan when it has been well browned and place it in a sieve with a plate underneath to catch any meat juices. Rinse and drain the rice and fry it gently in the skillet until it becomes glassy in appearance. Add the onion and garlic and proceed as in the recipe. Stir in the meat and any juices at the same time as the fruit and add a double quantity of broth as the rice will require more liquid. Stir occasionally during cooking so that the ingredients cook evenly.

Braised Duck with Red Cabbage

In Germany, braised duck with red cabbage is traditionally served with potato dumplings or plain boiled potatoes. The duck itself is stuffed with apples, chicken livers and herbs and braised in white wine.

Serves 4

4 slices white bread
without crusts
1 cup lukewarm milk
⅓ cup raisins
1 duck, weighing about
4 lb, with liver
5 oz chicken livers · 4 apples
6 tablespoons goose fat or lard · salt
freshly ground black pepper
2 sprigs fresh or
½ teaspoon dried marjoram
small bunch fresh parsley
1 egg · 1 stalk celery
1 carrot · 2 onions
1 cup dry white wine
1 head red cabbage
(about 2 lb)
1 tablespoon sugar
pinch ground allspice
1–2 small bay leaves
2 tablespoons wine vinegar
6 tablespoons water
2 tablespoons currant jelly

Preparation time: 2¼ hours

Place the bread in a bowl, pour the lukewarm milk over it and set aside for 15 minutes. Meanwhile, rinse the raisins in hot water and pat dry in a dish towel. Remove any skin, tubes or sinews from the duck liver and chicken livers. Pat dry and chop finely. Peel and core 1½ apples, and chop into small cubes.

Melt 2 tablespoons of the goose fat or lard in a skillet and fry the apples and livers over a moderate heat for 5 minutes. Remove from the pan and place in a bowl.

Squeeze the excess milk out of the bread and put the bread in the bowl with the liver and apple mixture. Add the raisins and salt and pepper to taste. Rinse the marjoram and half of the parsley, shake dry and chop very finely. Put the herbs in the bowl, add the egg and mix everything together thoroughly.

Rinse the duck in cold water and pat dry. Season the duck inside and out with salt and pepper, then stuff with the apple and liver mixture. Truss the duck by first pulling the skin around the vent opening

together and fastening the edges together with metal skewers or wooden toothpicks. When the skewers or toothpicks are in place, truss the duck by tying the string crosswise around the skewers or toothpicks, finishing with a firm knot. Melt 2 tablespoons of the goose fat or lard in a large saucepan and fry the duck until it is brown on all sides.

Meanwhile, trim the celery. Peel the carrot and one of the onions. Chop the vegetables coarsely. Add them to the pan with the duck and fry until they begin to take on color. Pour in the wine, cover the pan and simmer gently for about 1½ hours or until the duck is tender.

Once the duck is simmering, prepare the red cabbage. Remove any coarse outer leaves, cut in half and remove the

core. Shred finely, rinse and drain. Peel and core the remaining apples. Peel the remaining onion and chop finely. Heat the rest of the goose fat or lard in a saucepan and fry the onion gently until it is soft and golden. Add the shredded cabbage and fry gently, stirring from time to time, until it is almost soft and beginning to fall together. Season with the sugar, allspice, salt, pepper, bay leaves and wine vinegar. Add the water and stir in the apples. Bring to a boil, then cover the pan and simmer over a gentle heat until the cabbage is very tender.

When the duck is ready, take it out of the pan. Remove the trussing string and skewers or toothpicks and keep the duck warm while making the gravy. Skim off as much fat as possible from the stock, then strain it and return to the pan. Boil rapidly over a high heat to reduce. Once again, skim off as much fat as possible and season to taste with salt and pepper.

Stir the currant jelly into the red cabbage. Discard the bay leaves and place the cabbage on a large heated serving platter. Place the duck whole or carved on the bed of red cabbage. Garnish with the rest of the parsley and serve hot, with the gravy.

1 **Trussing the duck.** Pull the skin together around the vent and fasten the edges with metal skewers or wooden toothpicks. Tie the string around the skewers or toothpicks and across the vent.

2 **Cooking the red cabbage.** Stir in the pieces of apple and add the water at the same time. Bring to a boil, then cover and reduce the heat. Simmer until the cabbage is tender.

3 **Preparing the gravy.** Skim as much fat as possible from the stock, strain it and then boil down over a high heat. Skim off the fat again, and season with salt and pepper.

Chicken Breast with Figs

Chicken breast with figs, deep-fried in small parchment paper packages, can be served on many occasions – as an appetizer or hors d'oeuvre or as a snack during an informal party. They can also be served as a light main course accompanied by a tossed green salad and potato straws or rice.

Serves 4

2 whole chicken breasts,
each weighing ½ lb, without
skin and bones
6–8 dried figs
2 tablespoons white port
or dry sherry
5–6 tablespoons soy sauce
1 orange
cayenne pepper
freshly ground black pepper
salt
2 tablespoons cornstarch
parchment paper
oil for deep frying

To marinate: 2 hours
Preparation time: 45 minutes

Wipe the chicken breasts with a damp cloth, pat dry and cut into pieces about 1¾–2 inches in size. Rinse the figs under hot water, dry throughly and cut into slices.

To make the marinade, pour the port or sherry into a bowl and stir in 2 tablespoons of the soy sauce. Rinse the orange in hot water, dry thoroughly and grate about half the rind (not the white pith) into the bowl. Halve the orange and squeeze the juice from one half. Stir it into the port mixture and season to taste with cayenne pepper and black pepper but only a little salt since there is salt in the soy sauce. Place the chicken and figs in the bowl and turn them a few times in the marinade. Cover the bowl and set aside to marinate for 1½ hours.

Remove the figs from the marinade and set aside. In order to give the chicken a particularly tender crust when frying, take a little of the marinade from the bowl and mix it with the cornstarch, then stir this carefully into the marinade in the bowl. Cover the bowl again and leave the

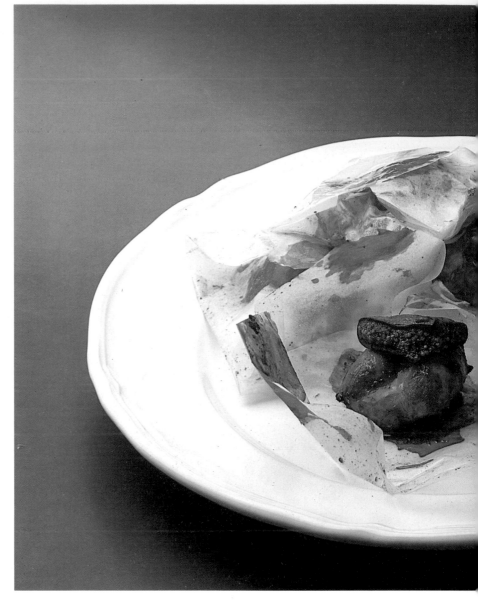

chicken pieces to marinate in this mixture for a further 30 minutes.

Prepare the paper cases by cutting out 5½ inch squares from parchment paper. Smooth them out on the work surface. Heat the oil to about 350°F in a deep fat fryer. If you do not have a deep frying thermometer, test the temperature of the oil by frying a cube of bread in it. If the cube turns brown in 10 seconds, then the oil has reached the correct temperature.

Drain the chicken pieces and pat them dry. Place one piece in the middle of every paper square and place a slice of fig on top. Brush the corners of the paper with the remaining soy sauce. Close the pack-

ages by folding over two opposite corners and pressing them firmly together. Now fold over the remaining corners and hold them firmly in your fingers until the paper sticks together.

Place a few packages at a time in the hot oil and fry for 5–7 minutes or until they are golden brown. Remove from the oil with a slotted spoon and place on a thick layer of paper towels to drain. Place on heated plates and serve immediately. Let your guests open the packages at the table so that none of the aroma is lost.

1 **Marinating the chicken and figs.** Place the chicken and figs in the marinade and turn to coat on all sides. Cover the bowl and marinate for 1½ hours before removing the figs.

2 **Preparing the paper packages.** Remove the chicken from the marinade, pat dry and place one piece in the middle of every paper square. Top with a slice of fig.

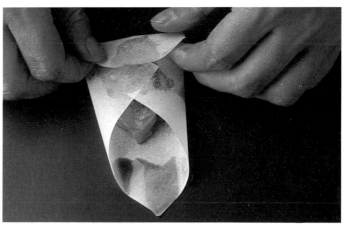

3 **Sealing the packages.** Brush the corners of the paper with soy sauce. Fold two opposite corners together and press firmly together. Fold over the remaining corners and press until they stick.

Coq au Vin de Bourgogne

There are many recipes for coq au vin – chicken cooked in wine – but coq au vin Burgundy style is one of the most delicious

Serves 4

1 plump roaster chicken,
weighing 3½ lb
salt
freshly ground white pepper
½ lb early carrots
½ lb scallions
½ lb small button mushrooms
1 stalk celery
1 carrot
3 oz piece slab bacon
2 tablespoons vegetable oil
3 tablespoons butter
3 cloves garlic
1 tablespoon flour
2 cups red
Burgundy wine
2 sprigs fresh or
½ teaspoon dried thyme
1 sprig fresh or
¼ teaspoon dried tarragon
small bunch fresh parsley
1 bay leaf
water or chicken broth
¼ lb chicken livers
2 tablespoons brandy
2 slices white bread

Preparation time: 2 hours

Rinse the chicken inside and out under cold running water and dry thoroughly. Divide into serving pieces. This is done as follows: remove the legs and thighs by bending them as far as possible from the body and separating them directly at the joint with a sharp knife or poultry shears. Separate the thigh from the drumstick by straightening the leg slightly and dividing it at the joint. Cut the wings off at the joint. Cut the body in half along the breastbone, then cut the two halves into two or three pieces crosswise. Dry the chicken pieces again and season with salt and pepper. Rub the seasoning in with the palm of your hand.

Preheat the oven to 350°F. Scrape the early carrots. Trim the scallions and put the green stalks on one side. Clean the mushrooms. Trim and finely chop the celery. Peel and dice the carrot. Cut the bacon into ½ inch cubes.

Heat the oil and 1 tablespoon of the butter in a large flameproof casserole. Fry the bacon until it is golden brown, then remove from the pot. Brown the white part of the scallions and the early carrots in the fat for 5 minutes, stirring frequently. Add the mushrooms and fry for a further 5 minutes. Remove the vegetables with a slotted spoon. Fry the chicken pieces, a few at a time, until they are golden on all sides.

Peel and chop the garlic and mix it with the chopped celery and carrot. Place these vegetables in the pot and fry until golden brown. Return the chicken pieces to the pot and sprinkle the flour over the chicken and vegetables. Continue to fry until the flour is well browned. Pour the red wine into the casserole, stir well and add the bacon, scallions, mushrooms and early carrots.

Rinse the thyme, tarragon and parsley and shake dry. Tie the herbs into a bunch together with the bay leaf. Place in the casserole and add enough water or broth so that everything is just half covered. Cover the casserole and place in the heated oven. Cook for 45 minutes.

Shortly before the end of cooking time, prepare the chicken livers. Pat them dry and chop very finely. Melt 1 tablespoon of the butter in a skillet and fry the livers for 30 seconds to 1 minute over a gentle heat. Press them through a sieve or purée in a blender or processor and mix with the brandy.

Remove the crusts from the bread and halve the slices diagonally. Melt the rest of the butter in the skillet and fry the bread until golden on both sides. Drain on paper towels.

Remove the chicken and vegetables from the casserole and keep warm. Discard the bunch of herbs and boil down the liquid on top of the range until it is well reduced. Remove the pot from the heat and stir in the liver and brandy mixture. Taste and adjust the seasoning. Put the chicken and vegetables back into the casserole and heat everything through again. Do not boil.

Rinse the green scallion stalks and chop them into thin rings. Serve the coq au vin garnished with the green scallion rings and triangles of fried bread.

1 **Removing the chicken legs.** Pull the leg as far as possible from the body and cut through the joint with a sharp knife or poultry shears. Repeat with the other leg.

2 **Cutting up the legs.** Straighten the leg and cut the thigh from the drumstick at the joint. Then remove the wings and cut the body in half lengthwise.

3 **Frying the vegetables.** Brown the white part of the scallions and early carrots in hot fat for 5 minutes, then add the mushrooms and continue frying.

4 **Adding the flour.** As soon as the diced vegetables have taken on color, sprinkle the flour over and let it brown. Add the red wine, vegetables and bacon.

Our tip

If you like garlic, rub the slices of bread with a little crushed garlic before frying them in butter or add a few chopped cloves of garlic to the skillet. Real garlic enthusiasts sprinkle finely chopped garlic on the bread after frying it.

Rabbit Stew

Mushrooms, vegetables and herbs give this spicy rabbit stew its wonderful flavor. It is easy to make and relatively low in calories.

Serves 4

1 frozen rabbit, weighing
2–2½ lb, cut up
2 tablespoons prepared mustard
2 tablespoons brandy
1 leek
2 onions
½ lb carrots
1 lb mixed mushrooms
(canned chanterelles and fresh
button mushrooms, for example)
1–2 cloves garlic
small bunch fresh parsley
2 sprigs fresh or
½ teaspoon dried thyme
1–2 leaves celery
3 tablespoons olive oil
1 tablespoon butter
¾ cup dry white wine
¾ cup hot chicken
or beef broth
salt
freshly ground black pepper
2 large ripe tomatoes
1 small bay leaf
2 dried juniper berries (optional)
1 clove
¼ cup heavy cream

To marinate: 30 minutes
Preparation time: 1½ hours

Allow the rabbit pieces to thaw. Wipe the pieces with a damp cloth and pat them dry. Stir the mustard and brandy together to make a smooth paste and brush the pieces all over with it. Cover and set aside to marinate for 30 minutes.

Trim the leek and cut on a slant into pieces ¾ inch wide. Put in a sieve and rinse to remove any grit that might remain. Put aside to drain.

Peel the onions and slice into thin rings. Peel the carrots. Cut into quarters lengthwise, then cut across into pieces ¾ inch wide. Clean fresh mushrooms (drain canned ones) and chop coarsely. Peel and finely chop the garlic. Rinse the parsley, thyme and celery leaves and shake dry.

Chop very finely.

Heat the oil and butter in a large flameproof casserole and fry the pieces of rabbit for 5–10 minutes over a high heat until they begin to brown. Add the vegetables to the casserole and fry, stirring frequently, until lightly browned. Add the herbs and garlic. Pour in about half the wine and bring to a boil, stirring all the time to loosen any meat sediments in the pan. Then add the rest of the wine and the broth and return to a boil. Boil for 1–2 minutes, then season to taste with salt and pepper.

Scald the tomatoes in boiling water for 10 seconds, then peel and remove the core and any pieces of hard stem. Halve the tomatoes so that all seed chambers are visible and, taking half a tomato at a time in the palm of your hand, squeeze gently until the seeds fall out. Discard the seeds. Chop the tomatoes coarsely. Put them in the casserole together with the bay leaf, juniper berries, the clove and any remaining mustard and brandy marinade. Reduce the heat, cover tightly and simmer over a gentle heat for 30–40 minutes.

Stir in the cream and simmer until the gravy has thickened a little. Season to taste with salt and pepper, discard the bay leaf, juniper berries and clove, and serve. Boiled noodles tossed in butter or boiled potatoes go well with this dish.

1 **Preparing the leek.** Trim off the root end and dark green leaves, then cut on a slant into pieces ¾ inch wide. Place in a sieve and rinse in cold water to remove any grit.

2 **Browning the vegetables.** Place the prepared vegetables in the casserole and brown them a little on all sides, stirring frequently. Add the garlic and herbs.

3 **Loosening the meat sediments.** Pour in about half the wine and bring to a boil, stirring all the time to loosen any meat sediments in the casserole. Add the rest of the wine and the broth.

Our tip

Rabbit is usually stewed because it is very lean and inclined to become dry if cooked in any other way. When you are browning the rabbit, make sure that it develops a thin crust which will protect the meat inside. Do not season the meat with salt before searing it as salt draws the juices out of meat. When stewing the rabbit, make sure that the casserole lid is tightly closed and that the stew does not boil. When the stew is ready the meat should be so tender that it practically falls from the bones.

Vol-au-Vent with Ragoût of Venison

It is not really as difficult as it looks to make a large pastry case, but peace and quiet and plenty of time are essential for success. It is also important to rest the case in a cool place before baking it. This allows the pastry to lose tension and ensures even rising.

Serves 8

2¼ lb frozen puff pastry
2 egg yolks
1 lb venison loin chops
5 oz fresh button mushrooms
juice ½ lemon
5 oz canned chanterelles or
other imported mushrooms
2 onions
2 carrots
2 cloves garlic
2 tablespoons butter
1 tablespoon vegetable oil
salt
freshly ground black pepper
1 tablespoon flour
6 tablespoons full-bodied
dry red wine
6 tablespoons hot beef broth
2 sprigs fresh or
½ teaspoon dried thyme
1 sprig fresh or
¼ teaspoon dried rosemary
1 juniper berry (optional)
1–2 teaspoons prepared mustard
5 oz broccoli florets
6 tablespoons heavy cream
small bunch fresh parsley

To thaw: about 30 minutes
Preparation time: 1½–2 hours

Spread out the sheets of pastry on a work surface and leave to thaw. Meanwhile, make the foil hemisphere which will be used to shape the pastry case. Line a round-bottomed bowl with aluminum foil. The edges of the foil should stand up above the rim of the bowl to a height of 4 inches. Pack the lined bowl with small pieces of parchment paper, then fold the edges of the foil over the top to form a hemisphere.

Brush half the sheets of pastry with cold water and place them on top of one another. Roll out the dough on a floured surface to ⅛ inch thick. Place the foil hemisphere, flat side down, in the center of the pastry. Cut around the foil shape leaving a margin 2½ inches wide. Then cut another circle 2½ inches away from the first circle. First remove the excess pastry, then carefully remove the 2½ inch wide pastry ring and put it aside for use later.

Roll out the remaining sheets of pastry in the same manner as before and lay the pastry over the foil hemisphere. Trim the edges and press lightly onto the pastry base. If necessary, brush the edges with water before pressing them together.

For the pastry case lid, cut out three or four pastry rings that diminish in size, in other words one large, one medium and two small (see photograph). Cut shapes from the excess pastry to decorate the sides of the pastry case.

Brush the entire surface with beaten egg yolk. Lay the rounds for the lid on top of one another, brushing each pastry round with egg yolk, and place them on top of the pastry case. Arrange the pastry decorations around the sides of the case. Brush the margin of pastry around the foil hemisphere with beaten egg yolk. Set aside to rest in a cool place for 15 minutes. Meanwhile, preheat the oven to 425°F.

Carefully transfer the pastry case to a dampened baking sheet. Place in the heated oven and bake for 20–25 minutes or until golden brown.

Meanwhile, prepare the ragoût. Remove any bones from the meat, then cut the meat into ½ inch cubes. Clean and chop fresh mushrooms and sprinkle with lemon juice to prevent discoloration. Drain and chop canned mushrooms. Peel the onions, carrots and garlic and chop them finely.

Heat the butter and oil in a large skillet. Brown the meat cubes well on all sides and remove from the pan. Fry the mushrooms in small portions, then remove from the pan and season to taste with salt and pepper. Fry the rest of the vegetables until golden brown, then sprinkle the flour over them. Fry, stirring, until the flour is browned. Pour in the wine and broth. Rinse, shake dry and chop the thyme and rosemary. Crush the juniper berry. Place the herbs and juniper berry in the pan and season with the mustard. Return the meat cubes to the pan. Bring to a boil and simmer for 20 minutes.

Meanwhile, cook the broccoli in boiling salted water for 3 minutes. Drain well and chop the broccoli into smaller pieces. Add to the pan with the cream. Stir well, then add the mushrooms. Boil down the liquid until it is creamy. Rinse,

shake dry and chop the parsley. Stir into the ragoût and keep warm.

Remove the pastry case from the oven. Use the largest pastry cutter (with which the largest pastry round for the lid was made) and a pointed knife to remove the lid. The paper must now be removed from the pastry case. This is done by leaving the pastry cutter in the pastry to act as a chimney and pulling out the pieces of paper and foil carefully through it. In this way the pastry will not be damaged.

Season the ragoût with salt and pepper to taste and pour it into the pastry case through the pastry cutter chimney. Remove the cutter, put on the lid and serve the vol-au-vent.

1 **Cutting out the circles.** Cut two circles around the foil hemisphere with $2\frac{1}{2}$ inches distance between them, and $2\frac{1}{2}$ inches between the first circle and the foil shape. Put the excess pastry and the pastry ring aside for later use.

2 **Shaping the pastry case.** Roll out the remaining pastry, lay it over the hemisphere and trim the edges. Press lightly onto the pastry base, first moistening if necessary.

3 **Putting the pastry ring in place.** Brush the margin with beaten egg yolk and lay the pastry ring on top. Press it down lightly and brush with more egg yolk.

4 **Removing the paper.** Remove the lid with the pastry cutter and a sharp knife. Leave the pastry cutter in place and pull the paper and foil out of the case.

Stuffed Pheasant with Cider Sauce

Apples are often used to give a fresh fruity sauce to game. In this recipe the apple flavor is intensified by the addition of Calvados and dry cider.

½ stale roll
¼ lb chicken livers
4 bacon slices
1½ onions · 5 Granny Smith apples
¼ lemon · salt
freshly ground black pepper
small bunch fresh parsley
1 egg yolk
1 pheasant, weighing
1¾ lb, dressed
4–8 slices salt pork or bacon
3 tablespoons butter
1 tablespoon vegetable oil
1 cup dry hard cider
1 tablespoon Calvados or applejack
2 tablespoons heavy cream

Preparation time: 1¼ hours

To make the stuffing, cut the roll into slices and soak in lukewarm water for 5 minutes. Meanwhile, clean the chicken livers. Chop the bacon. Peel the half onion and one of the apples. Cut both into quarters and core the apple. Grind the livers, bacon, onion and apple finely or process in a food processor. Place in a bowl.

Squeeze the excess water from the bread. Tear the bread into pieces and place in the bowl. Rinse the lemon with hot water, pat dry and grate the rind into the bowl. Season to taste with salt and pepper. Rinse the parsley, shake it dry and chop finely. Place in the bowl. Add the egg yolk and mix everything together well.

Preheat the oven to 425°F. Rinse the pheasant inside and out under cold running water. Dry thoroughly and season lightly inside with salt and pepper. Stuff the pheasant and sew up the vent. To truss the pheasant, lay a long piece of string under the tail, cross the string over the front of the tail and bind an end around each leg. Pull the ends tightly and turn the pheasant over without letting go of the string. Run the string along one side of the bird, over the thigh and wing, right across the neck to bind the other wing before securing with a firm knot. Bard the pheasant on all sides with the salt pork or bacon slices and truss it again to keep the fat in place.

Peel the remaining onion and two of the apples. Core the apples, then chop the apples and onion.

Heat a roasting pan on top of the stove. Place the pheasant in the pan, breast down. The fat from the barding should soon start to run. Fry, turning, until the barding fat is crisp, then add 1 tablespoon of the butter and the oil to the pan and place the chopped apples and onion around the pheasant. Fry, stirring, until they begin to take on color. Turn the pheasant breast up. Add the cider and Calvados and bring to a boil, stirring to loosen any sediments in the pan. Cover the pan and place in the heated oven. Roast for 35 minutes, basting the pheasant frequently with the juices in the pan.

Take the pan from the oven and remove the trussing strings and barding fat from the pheasant. Spread 1 tablespoon of the butter over the breast. Place in the oven again, without the lid, and let the pheasant brown for a further 10 minutes. Remove from the pan, cover with foil and keep warm.

Strain the stock through a fine sieve into a saucepan and skim off any fat. Stir in the cream and boil to reduce the sauce until it is creamy in consistency. Taste and adjust the seasoning, and keep warm.

Peel and core the remaining apples and cut across into rings. Heat the remaining butter in a skillet and fry the rings until they are golden on both sides. Place on paper towels to drain.

Serve the pheasant garnished with the apple rings. Serve the sauce separately.

1 **Trussing the pheasant.** Lay a long piece of string under the tail, cross it over at the front and bind an end around each leg. Pull the string tightly and turn the pheasant over.

2 **Frying the apples and onions.** Melt 1 tablespoon of the butter and the oil in the roasting pan, add the chopped apples and onions and fry gently until they are golden brown.

3 **Frying the apple rings.** Melt the rest of the butter in a skillet and fry the apple rings until they are golden on both sides. Drain off the fat on paper towels.

Chicken Baked in Clay

Chicken baked in clay is more than just an amazing presentation. The clay seals in the juices and flavors resulting in an unusually delicious and succulent dish. Although fun for a summer barbecue, the recipe will be equally successful if the chicken is cooked in aluminium foil or an unglazed earthenware pot.

Serves 4

---

10 bunches assorted fresh herbs
(such as parsley, thyme, rosemary,
sage, tarragon)
2–4 cloves garlic
$\frac{1}{2}$ lemon
1 plump roaster chicken,
weighing about $3\frac{1}{2}$ lb
salt
freshly ground white pepper
2 tablespoons butter, softened
about 9 lb fresh damp clay
(obtainable at arts and crafts stores)

Preparation time: at least 2 hours

Before preparing the chicken, light the charcoal in the barbecue in which the chicken is to be baked. The charcoal must be at least 4 inches deep. Make a good fire and leave to burn until covered with gray ash and the coals glow red when blown on.

Rinse the bunches of herbs, shake them thoroughly dry and mix them well. If they are not well mixed, the chicken may well taste strongly of thyme on one side and tarragon on the other. Peel the cloves of garlic, slice them thinly and mix them with the herbs. Rinse the lemon under hot water, dry thoroughly and grate off the rind.

Rinse the chicken inside and out under cold running water. Dry thoroughly. Rub the chicken inside and out with salt, pepper and the grated lemon rind. Spread the butter over the chicken or chop it into small pieces and place inside the chicken.

Cover the work surface with a large sheet of thick plastic wrap or a plastic garbage bag which has been cut open. (It would be difficult to lift the heavy clay from the surface without the plastic.) Place the clay in the middle of the plastic sheet. Wet your hands and push the clay from the center towards the edges of the plastic sheet until you have a large flat round of clay about 1 inch thick. It should be large enough to wrap around the chicken. Wet your hands again and smooth over the surface of the clay until there are no cracks to be seen and the surface is quite smooth.

Lay one-third of the herbs in the center of the clay round and place the chicken on top. Arrange the rest of the herbs over the chicken so that it is completely covered. Use the foil to lift the clay from the work surface and wrap it over the chicken. Press the edges of the clay together with wet hands and rub over the seams until they are quite smooth. During this process try to avoid stretching or pulling the clay as this might result in cracks on some parts of the clay shell being thinner than the rest. It is important that the clay is equally thick all over to ensure even cooking.

Place the clay parcel in the glowing fire and heap up some of the hot charcoal around the edges. The chicken will take $1\frac{1}{2}$ hours to bake.

When it is ready, remove the clay parcel from the fire with flameproof gloves. Place it on a thick board and use a hammer to crack it open; it will be as hard as stone. Remove the pieces of clay carefully so that they do not crumble over the chicken. If any small pieces of clay do fall on the chicken, brush them off with a pastry brush. Remove the herbs from the chicken and serve immediately.

Our tip

Crack the clay open at the table to surprise your guests. Place the board on a small side-table so that you have enough room. Hit the clay with care, but not too gently, or small pieces will fall off and tumble into the herbs and chicken. It is possible to avoid this altogether by laying a sheet of parchment paper between the herbs and the clay.

1 **Covering the chicken with herbs.** Place one-third of the herbs in the center of the clay round and lay the chicken on top of them. Cover with the rest of the herbs.

2 **Wrapping up the chicken.** Lift the clay from the work surface with the help of the plastic sheet. Wrap it carefully around the chicken and seal it with wet hands.

3 **Baking the chicken.** Place the clay parcel on the thick bed of glowing charcoal. Heap up some of the charcoal around the edges and bake for 1½ hours.

4 **Opening the clay parcel.** Remove the clay from the fire with flameproof gloves, place it on a board and crack it open with a hammer. Remove the clay carefully.

Sweet and Sour Chicken

Sweet and sour chicken must be served very quickly or the vegetables and the crisp batter around the chicken may become soft. Boiled rice and warm sake are the traditional accompaniments.

Serves 4

1¼ lb chicken breasts,
without skin and bone
1 egg
¼ cup flour
¼ cup cornstarch
salt
freshly ground white pepper
2 tablespoons soy sauce
2 tablespoons rice wine
or dry sherry
1 cup cold chicken broth
1 green pepper
2 carrots
1 leek
1 onion
1 head Chinese cabbage
(about 5 oz)
4 slices canned pineapple
1–2 cloves garlic
peanut or vegetable oil
for deep frying
2 tablespoons peanut oil
1½ tablespoons sugar
2–3 tablespoons red wine
vinegar
1–2 tablespoons tomato
catsup

Preparation time: 1 hour

Pat the chicken breasts dry with paper towels and cut them into pieces about 1 inch in size.

Separate the egg and set the white aside. Place the egg yolk, flour and cornstarch in a bowl and season with salt and pepper. Add 1 tablespoon of the soy sauce and rice wine or sherry and a little of the chicken broth and mix to a smooth batter. It should not be too thin. Set aside for 30 minutes.

Meanwhile, prepare the vegetables. Halve the green pepper, remove the seeds and core and cut into pieces ¾ inch in size. Peel the carrots and score notches in them lengthwise. Cut them into slices; these will be flower-shaped. Trim the leek, halve lengthwise and rinse thoroughly under cold running water. Drain and cut into ¾ inch lengths. Peel the onion and cut into quarters. Pull the layers of onion apart. Rinse the cabbage, drain and cut into pieces ¾ inch in size. Drain the pineapple slices and chop into ¾ inch pieces as well. Peel the garlic and chop finely or crush.

Heat the oil in a deep fat fryer to 350°F. Preheat the oven to 250°F. Place a baking sheet in the oven to heat at the same time.

Beat the egg white to stiff peaks, then fold it loosely into the batter. Place the chicken pieces in the batter, a few at a time. Turn the chicken pieces in the batter, then deep fry in portions until golden brown. Drain on paper towels and place on the baking sheets in the heated oven to keep warm while the remaining chicken is fried.

Heat 2 tablespoons of peanut oil in a skillet and stir-fry the carrots, green peppers, leek, onion, cabbage and garlic over a high heat for about 5 minutes. The vegetables should become golden but not brown. Sprinkle the sugar over the vegetables and as soon as it has melted and become golden brown, add the wine vinegar, the rest of the chicken broth and the tomato catsup. Stir in the pineapple pieces and cook over a high heat for 1–2 minutes. Season to taste with salt and pepper and add the remaining soy sauce and rice wine or sherry. Add the fried chicken pieces and mix in quickly. Serve immediately before the vegetables or chicken can go soft.

1 **Slicing the carrots.** Peel the carrots and score them lengthwise with three or four notches before cutting them into slices which will be flower-shaped.

2 **Frying the chicken.** Coat the chicken pieces in the batter and fry in portions until the pieces are golden brown. Drain on paper towels and keep warm.

3 **Adding the broth.** As soon as the sugar melts and becomes golden brown, add the wine vinegar, the rest of the broth and the catsup. Stir in the pineapple pieces.

4 **Stirring in the chicken.** Stir the fried chicken pieces quickly into the vegetables. Serve immediately so there is no time for the batter on the chicken to soften.

Our tip

The preparation is of utmost importance in this recipe as all the ingredients should retain a certain crispness. Fry the chicken in small portions so that the batter becomes crisp and place the pieces next to one another on the baking sheet in the oven and not on top of one another, otherwise the crisp batter will become soft. Mix the chicken with the vegetables quickly and serve immediately.

Hazelnut Pudding with Chocolate Sauce

Old-fashioned desserts are often the ones that everybody loves best. This hazelnut pudding is an excellent example of a steamed pudding – juicy, light and delicately fluffy, and with a melting sweetness which is irresistible.

Serves 8

---

1 cup shelled hazelnuts
4 macaroons (about 1 oz)
1 vanilla bean
5 tablespoons sugar
2 eggs
1 tablespoon amaretto
(almond liqueur)
pinch salt
6 tablespoons flour
pinch baking powder
2 tablespoons butter
butter for greasing mold
1 tablespoon fine soft
bread crumbs
4 squares (1 oz each)
semisweet chocolate
$\frac{3}{4}$ cup heavy cream

Preparation time: $1\frac{1}{2}$ hours

Preheat the oven to 425°F. Spread out the hazelnuts on a baking sheet and toast them in the heated oven until the skins begin to split. This will take 8–10 minutes, depending on the age of the nuts. Remove from the oven and pour the nuts from the sheet onto a dish towel. Rub them in the towel until the skins fall off, then spread them out and leave to cool.

Put the macaroons in a plastic bag and crush them finely with a rolling pin or grind them in a food processor. Place the vanilla bean on the work surface and, holding it firmly, slit it open lengthwise. Scrape out the vanilla seeds and pulp with the tip of a sharp knife. Mix 3 tablespoons of the sugar with the seeds and pulp. When the hazelnuts have cooled, grind them in a nut mill or food processor. Put aside 1 tablespoon of the ground nuts for use later.

Separate the eggs into two bowls: the whites into a large one and the yolks into a smaller one. Beat the egg yolks and amaretto together until frothy. Gradually add the vanilla and sugar mixture and continue beating until the mixture is pale and creamy. Beat the egg whites with the salt until stiff peaks form. Gradually add the remaining sugar, beating constantly. Spoon the egg white mixture onto the egg yolk mixture. Sift the flour and baking powder over the egg white mixture in the bowl. Add the ground hazelnuts and crushed macaroons and fold everything gently but thoroughly together with a metal spoon or spatula.

Melt the butter over a gentle heat; do not let it brown. Remove from the heat and cool to lukewarm, then pour it into the hazelnut mixture in a thin stream. Fold it in lightly.

Grease a 1 quart steaming mold thickly with butter. Mix the bread crumbs with the reserved tablespoon of ground hazelnuts and sprinkle them over the sides of the mold. Pour the hazelnut mixture into the mold – it should not be more than three-quarters full. Cover tightly with a lid, or greased parchment paper and foil tied on securely with string.

Place the mold in a steamer or deep, narrow-sided saucepan and pour enough boiling water into the pan to come three-quarters of the way up the sides of the mold. Cover and simmer gently for 1 hour, adding more water when necessary. Do not let the water boil.

Shortly before the end of cooking time, break the chocolate into pieces and place in a heavy saucepan (or the top of a double boiler) with the cream. Stir constantly over a gentle heat until the chocolate has melted and blended with the cream.

Remove the lid from the steaming mold and wait for a few seconds for the steam to rise from the pudding before unmolding it onto a serving plate. Pour the chocolate sauce over the pudding and serve immediately. If any of the pudding is left over, it can be served cold as cake.

1 **Skinning the hazelnuts.** Toast the nuts in a heated oven, then rub off the brown skins in a dish towel. Spread out the nuts and leave to cool before grinding.

2 **Removing the vanilla pulp.** Slit open the vanilla bean lengthwise and scrape out the seeds and pulp with the point of a knife. Mix the seeds and pulp with sugar.

3 **Folding in the butter.** Pour the cooled melted butter into the hazelnut mixture in a thin stream. Fold in gently, then pour into the prepared mold.

Honey Parfait with Strawberry Sauce

Frozen custards are among the finest and creamiest iced desserts. Try this unusual combination of sweet honey parfait with a delicately tart strawberry sauce.

Serves 4

1 egg
1 egg yolk
2 tablespoons sugar
3 tablespoons acacia or
clover honey
1 cup heavy cream
1–2 tablespoons framboise
or Kirsch

For the strawberry sauce:
1 cup unsweetened
strawberry purée, sieved
1–1$\frac{1}{2}$ tablespoons sugar or
to taste
juice $\frac{1}{2}$ lemon
2 tablespoons framboise
or Kirsch

Preparation time: 30 minutes
To chill: 2–2$\frac{1}{2}$ hours

Place the egg and the egg yolk in a bowl and beat them until they are pale and frothy. Gradually add the sugar, beating all the time. When the mixture has the consistency of thick cream, beat in the honey. Continue beating until the mixture is very light and frothy. Do not stop beating until you have reached this stage.

Pour the cream into another bowl and whip until it is thick. Spoon the cream onto the surface of the egg mixture and fold it in very gently. Do not stir. Fold in the framboise or Kirsch. Pour the parfait mixture into four freezerproof molds, each with a capacity of $\frac{1}{2}$–$\frac{3}{4}$ cup. Smooth over the surface of the mixture, cover and place in the freezer. Freeze for 2–2$\frac{1}{2}$ hours. After this time the parfaits should be firm but not hard.

To make the sauce, mix the strawberry purée with the sugar and lemon juice. Cover and put aside for the sugar to dissolve and pervade the mixture. Add the framboise or Kirsch just before serving.

Dip the molds in hot water for a few seconds, then unmold the parfaits onto individual plates. Pour a little sauce over each one and serve immediately.

1 **Adding the honey.** Pour the honey into the egg mixture, beating all the time. Continue beating until the mixture is very light and frothy. Do not stop beating until this stage is reached.

2 **Folding in the cream.** Fold the whipped cream into the mixture gently. Do not stir. Add the framboise or Kirsch at the final stage of folding.

3 **Filling the molds.** Pour the mixture into four freezerproof molds, each with a capacity of $\frac{1}{2}-\frac{3}{4}$ cup. Smooth over the surface and freeze for $2-2\frac{1}{2}$ hours.

4 **Unmolding the parfaits.** Dip the molds in hot water for a few seconds then turn them over onto individual plates. Pour a little sauce over each parfait and serve.

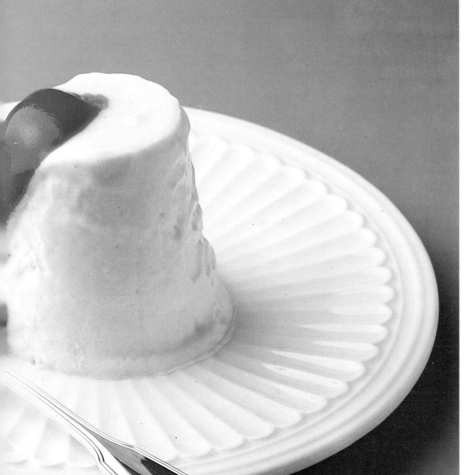

Our tip

Restaurants use small metal molds for parfaits because they quickly become very cold. If you do not have appropriate molds, use plastic yogurt tubs or freezerproof cups. If you make the parfait the day before you intend to serve it, remove the molds from the freezer an hour before serving and place in the refrigerator to thaw slightly.

Clafoutis aux Cerises

A clafoutis is a cross between a thick pudding and a fruity pancake. It can be served for brunch or afternoon tea as well as dessert.

Serves 4

2 lb dark sweet
cherries, fresh or frozen
6 tablespoons flour
pinch salt
2 tablespoons vanilla sugar (see below)
6 tablespoons sugar
3 eggs
6 tablespoons milk
2 tablespoons Kirsch
butter for greasing dish
fine soft bread crumbs for
lining dish
$\frac{1}{2}$–$\frac{3}{4}$ cup confectioners' sugar

Preparation time: 45 minutes

Rinse the fresh cherries and drain them on a thick layer of paper towels or pat them dry in a dish towel. Thaw frozen cherries. Remove the stalks and stones. Preheat the oven to 400°F.

Sift the flour into a bowl. Add the salt and the vanilla and plain sugars. Mix everything well together.

Break the eggs into another bowl and beat them with a fork until the yolks have completely combined with the whites. Beat the milk into the mixture. Pour the egg and milk mixture gradually into the flour mixture, beating all the time until the mixture is quite smooth. Add the Kirsch. Pass the cake batter through a sieve into another bowl to remove any lumps of flour or egg white.

Generously butter an 8 inch diameter soufflé or other dish. Sprinkle the bread crumbs over the bottom and sides of the dish. Place the cherries in the dish, then pour the cake batter evenly over them. The cherries should be almost covered. Sprinkle the top so thickly with sifted confectioners' sugar that the cherries can hardly be seen.

Place in the heated oven and bake for 25–30 minutes until set. Remove from the oven and sprinkle generously with sifted confectioners' sugar once more. Serve hot or cold.

Vanilla sugar To make vanilla sugar place about 6 vanilla pods upright in a deep glass storage jar and fill it with sugar. After a few days the sugar will have become impregnated with the vanilla flavor and will be ready for use.

1 **Straining the batter.** Beat the cake batter until quite smooth, then strain through a sieve into another bowl to remove any lumps of flour or egg white.

2 **Filling the dish.** Place the cherries in the prepared baking dish and pour the cake batter over them as evenly as possible. The cherries should be almost covered.

3 **Covering with confectioners' sugar.** Sift the confectioners' sugar thickly over the pudding so that the cherries can hardly be seen. Place in the heated oven and bake until set.

Our tip

In France clafoutis is generally made from fresh dark juicy cherries – never with canned or bottled fruit. However, if cherries are not in season, the recipe can be made with ripe plums such as greengages, Stanleys or damsons. The quality of the fruit is decisive for the fresh flavor of the dessert. In order to intensify the fruit flavor you might like to add a little of the appropriate fruit liqueur.

Crème Caramel

Crème caramel is a delicious combination of creamy vanilla custard and caramel sauce. It is suprising that this dessert has the reputation of being difficult to make. It is not difficult, but it is important to prepare everything beforehand so that the various stages can follow one another in the right order fairly quickly.

Serves 6

¾ cup sugar
4 tablespoons water
1 cup milk
6 tablespoons heavy cream
1 vanilla bean
2 eggs plus 2 egg yolks
pinch salt
5 tablespoons sugar
butter for greasing paper

Preparation time: 1½ hours
To chill: at least 4 hours

First prepare the lids for six individual molds of about ½ cup capacity. Cut out rounds of parchment paper about ½ inch larger than the tops of the molds. An easy way to do this is to cut out squares of paper larger than the diameter of the molds. Fold them in half diagonally, then fold the resulting triangle in half. Trim the corners to produce paper rounds when they are unfolded.

Preheat the oven to 300°F. Put the sugar and water in a small saucepan and heat gently, stirring until the sugar dissolves. Bring to a boil and boil, stirring constantly, until the resulting syrup is golden brown. Remove the pan from the heat and pour the caramel into the molds. It becomes hard very quickly so it is important to do this as fast as possible. Pour hot water into the cooking pan immediately so that it will be easier to wash later.

Pour the milk and cream into a heavy saucepan. Split open the vanilla bean lengthwise and scrape out the seeds and pulp with a sharp knife. Place the seeds, pulp and bean in the pan with the milk and heat until the milk has almost reached boiling point. Remove the pan from the heat and strain to discard the vanilla bean.

Beat the eggs and egg yolk together. Gradually add the salt and sugar, beating constantly. As soon as the mixture becomes very frothy, pour in the hot milk mixture in a thin stream, beating constantly, then leave to stand for 10 minutes. Skim the foam from the top of the custard using a spoon or ladle (this will prevent bubbles forming later). Pour the custard into the molds. Grease one side of the paper lids with butter and place them, buttered side down, on the molds. Press the edges down firmly and tie on with string, if necessary.

Place a thick layer of brown paper on the bottom of a baking pan and stand the molds on it. Pour enough boiling water into the pan from the side to come halfway up the sides of the molds. Place in the heated oven immediately and bake for about 1 hour.

Remove the molds from the pan and allow to cool, then chill for at least 4 hours. To serve, unmold onto individual serving plates.

1 **Making the caramel.** Dissolve the sugar cubes in the water in a small saucepan and bring to a boil. Boil, stirring constantly, until the syrup is golden.

2 **Pouring the caramel into the molds.** Remove the pan from the heat and pour the caramel into the molds immediately, otherwise it will begin to harden.

3 **Skimming off the foam.** Skim the foam from the surface of the custard with a spoon or ladle, to prevent bubbles forming later. Pour the custard into the molds.

4 **Covering the molds.** Place the parchment paper lids, buttered side down, on the molds and press the edges down firmly. Tie with string, if necessary.

Puffs with Raspberry Sauce

Light-as-air puffs filled with cream and covered with raspberry sauce can be served as dessert or for afternoon tea.

Serves 4

---

1 cup flour
½ cup water
pinch salt
3 tablespoons butter
2–3 eggs (depending on size)
butter and flour for
baking sheet
1 pint fresh or frozen
raspberries (about ¾ lb)
3 tablespoons sugar
1 teaspoon lemon juice
2 tablespoons framboise or brandy
1½ cups whipping cream
1½ tablespoons vanilla sugar
(see page 142)

To cool: 1¼ hours
Preparation time: 1 hour

Preheat the oven to 425°F. Sift the flour onto a sheet of wax paper. Place the water, salt and butter in a saucepan and heat until the butter has melted and the mixture begins to boil rapidly. Remove from the heat and pour the flour all at once into the still boiling liquid. Quickly stir the mixture together with a wooden spoon, then place the saucepan back on the heat. Continue to stir vigorously until the mixture is thoroughly combined and a white skin begins to form on the bottom of the pan. Remove from the heat, transfer to a bowl and beat in one egg. Set aside to cool. When it is lukewarm, beat in a second egg. Take a little of the paste on the end of the wooden spoon and hold it over the bowl. It should be shiny and smooth and hang from the spoon like long icicles. If it does not, add the remaining egg – or half an egg – and beat it into the paste thoroughly. (If very large eggs are used, it may be possible to do without the third egg.) Stop beating as soon as a pliable consistency is obtained; if the paste becomes too soft it will not rise as much as it should.

Grease a baking sheet with butter and dredge it with flour. To form the puffs, place the paste in a pastry bag fitted with a star-shaped tube. Hold the bag directly over the baking sheet and press out small high mounds about the size of a walnut. Leave a good deal of space between the mounds so that they can spread.

Place the baking sheet at once in the heated oven and bake the puffs for about 20 minutes. Do not open the oven door during the first 10–15 minutes of cooking or the puffs will collapse. Remove the baking sheet from the oven. Slit open the puffs with a pair of kitchen scissors or the tip of a sharp knife. This will allow the steam trapped inside to escape. Place on a wire rack to cool.

Meanwhile, make the raspberry sauce. Place the raspberries in a bowl with the sugar, lemon juice and half the framboise or brandy. If using frozen raspberries, leave them to thaw. Mix the ingredients together. Place a sieve over a saucepan and press the fruit mixture through it using the back of a spoon to rub it through. Bring the purée to a boil, stirring all the time, and simmer until the mixture has been reduced to a syrupy consistency. Remove from the heat. Leave it to cool, then add the rest of the framboise or brandy to taste.

Whip the cream until it is stiff and sweeten it with the vanilla sugar. Place in a pastry bag fitted with the star-shaped tube and fill the puffs. Pour the raspberry sauce over them and serve immediately so that they will not become soft.

1 Combining the mixture. Stir vigorously over heat until the flour is combined with the melted mixture. Transfer the paste to a bowl and beat in the eggs one at a time.

2 Testing the paste. Take some of the paste on the end of the wooden spoon and hold it over the bowl. It should be smooth and shiny and hang from the spoon like icicles.

3 Forming the puffs. Hold the pastry bag over the baking sheet and press out small mounds the size of a walnut. Leave enough space between them. Place in the oven.

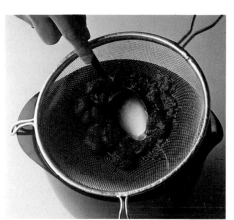

4 Making the sauce. Press the raspberries through a fine sieve placed over a saucepan, using the back of a spoon. Simmer until the sauce is syrupy.

Charlotte Royale

Charlotte royale may not be one of the quickest of desserts to prepare, but it is surely one of the most delicious.

Serves 8

For the jelly roll:
butter for greasing pan · 4 eggs
3 tablespoon cold water
6 tablespoons sugar
1 lemon · pinch salt
1 cup flour
sugar for sprinkling
1 jar (about 1 lb)
currant jelly

For the wine cream:
1 envelope unflavored gelatin
3 tablespoons boiling water
3 eggs
6 tablespoons sugar
1 cup full-bodied
dry white wine
2 tablespoons brandy · pinch salt
1¼ cups whipping cream

Preparation time: 1 hour
To chill: 5–6 hours

Preheat the oven to 400°F. Line a 12 × 8 inch jelly roll pan with parchment paper that has been greased with butter.

Separate the eggs into two bowls: the whites into a large one and the yolks in a smaller one. Beat the egg yolks with the water until they are frothy, then gradually beat in ¼ cup of the sugar. Beat until the mixture is white and frothy.

Rinse the lemon under hot water and pat it dry. Grate off the yellow rind from one half very finely, taking care not to grate the bitter white pith. Set the other half of the lemon aside.

Beat the egg whites with the salt to stiff peaks in the other bowl. Add the remaining sugar, beating constantly. Spoon the egg whites onto the surface of the egg yolk mixture. Sift the flour over the top, sprinkle over the grated lemon rind and fold all together gently. Spread the cake batter in the prepared pan. Place in the heated oven and bake for about 12 minutes.

Meanwhile, spread a clean dish towel on the work surface and sprinkle it generously with sugar. Stir the currant jelly until it is smooth, heating it slightly if necessary.

Turn out the cake onto the towel. Brush the parchment paper with cold water, then peel it off carefully. Brush the currant jelly over the cake immediately, leaving a clear border of ½ inch on all sides. Roll up the cake from a long side, lifting the edges of the towel to help roll. Leave to cool.

To make the the wine cream filling, sprinkle the gelatin over the water in a small cup and stir until dissolved. Grate the rind finely from the reserved half of lemon and squeeze out the juice. Separate the eggs. Beat the egg yolks until they are frothy and add the sugar and wine gradually. Add the lemon rind and juice and the brandy. Stir 3 tablespoons of the wine mixture into the dissolved gelatin, then add to the remaining wine mixture and combine thoroughly. Chill until the mixture has thickened to the consistency of unbeaten egg whites. Beat the egg whites with the salt to stiff peaks. Whip the cream in another bowl until it is thick. Fold the cream thoroughly into the wine mixture, then gently fold in the egg whites.

Cut the jelly roll into slices about ⅛ inch thick. Carefully line a deep round-bottomed bowl or mold that has a 2 quart capacity with the cake slices, pressing them gently together so that they cannot fall off. Wrap any leftover cake slices in plastic wrap or foil and serve on another occasion. Pour in the wine cream.

Chill for 4–5 hours or until the cream is set, then unmold onto a serving dish and serve immediately. The charlotte is best served cut in slices like a fruit pie or cake.

1 **Rolling up the cake.** Lift the edges of the dish towel and roll up the warm cake from a long side. Leave the towel over the jelly roll to prevent it from unrolling, and allow to cool.

2 **Mixing the gelatin** with the wine and egg mixture. When the gelatin is dissolved, add 3 tablespoons of the wine and egg mixture and stir until they are combined.

3 **Filling the mold.** Line the bottom and sides of a deep round-bottomed bowl or mold with jelly roll slices and then pour in the wine cream. Chill until set.

Tarte aux Poires

This excellent French fruit tart is delightfully juicy and tastes strongly of butter.

For the pastry:
2 cups flour
1 small egg
pinch salt
½ cup sugar
½ cup cold butter
1 lemon

For the filling:
2½ lb Bartlett or Bosc pears
juice 1 lemon
3 tablespoons butter
5 tablespoons sugar
¼ cup dry white wine
1 tablespoon amaretto
¼ cup ground almonds
½ cup fine soft bread crumbs
⅓ cup blanched almonds
¼ cup confectioners' sugar

Preparation time: 1 hour
To cool: 30 minutes

First make the pastry. Sift the flour onto a work surface and make a well in the center. Add the egg and salt to the well and sprinkle the sugar over the egg. Cut the butter into small pieces and place all around the edges of the flour. Rinse the lemon under hot water, dry it thoroughly and grate the rind over the other ingredients. Knead the ingredients together to form a smooth dough, using your fingertips. Knead as quickly as possible so that the ingredients, particularly the butter, do not become warm. If they do, the resulting pastry may be heavy. Roll the dough into a ball, wrap in foil and place it in the refrigerator to rest for 30 minutes.

Meanwhile, prepare the filling. Peel and core the pears and cut lengthwise into thin, even-sized slices. Sprinkle the slices with lemon juice to prevent them from going brown. Heat the butter in a saucepan and add the pears, sugar, white wine and amaretto. Cover the pan and bring slowly to a boil, shaking the pan frequently. As soon as the mixture begins to boil, reduce the temperature and remove the lid from the pan. Cook, shaking the pan frequently, until the pears are glassy in appearance and the liquid has evaporated. Set aside to cool.

Preheat the oven to 400°F. Remove the dough from the refrigerator and roll it out into a round on a floured surface. The dough should be about ⅛ inch thick. Roll the dough loosely around the rolling pin and unroll it over a 9 inch quiche or tart pan. Press it into the pan and trim the edges with a knife. Any excess dough can be distributed over the bottom of the case; smooth it onto the rest of the dough with the fingers. Prick the dough with a fork so that no bubbles form while it is baking.

Mix the ground almonds with the bread crumbs and spread evenly over the bottom of the pastry case. Place the cooled pears on top. Slice the blanched almonds and sprinkle over the top. Place in the heated oven and bake for 25–30 minutes.

Remove the tart from the oven and sift a thick layer of confectioners' sugar over the surface while it is still very hot. Let it cool, and serve lukewarm or cold.

1 **Mixing the dough.** Cut the butter into small pieces and place around the edges of the flour. Grate the lemon rind over it. Knead into the flour with the egg and sugar.

2 **Kneading the dough.** Take the dough between your two outstretched palms and press it firmly. Do this as quickly as possible to prevent the dough becoming warm.

3 **Lining the tart pan.** Roll the dough loosely around the rolling pin and roll it out over the tart pan. Press it gently into place with your fingers and trim the edges.

4 **Filling the pastry case.** Sprinkle the bread crumbs and ground almonds evenly over the bottom of the pastry case. Cover with the cooled pears and sprinkle with sliced almonds.

Salzburg Dumplings

Salzburg dumplings are as much a distinctive feature of Austria as the Prater pleasure park with its big wheel in Vienna. They are not, of course, dumplings of the usual kind, but are a sweet soufflé traditionally baked in three mounds in an oval dish.

Serves 4

½ lemon
4 eggs
pinch salt
2 tablespoons sugar
1 tablespoon vanilla sugar
(see page 142)
2 tablespoons flour
2 tablespoons butter
confectioners' sugar

Preparation time: 30 minutes

Preheat the oven to 400°F. Rinse the lemon under hot water and pat it dry. Grate off the yellow rind very finely, taking care not to grate the bitter-tasting white pith.

Separate the eggs into two bowls: the whites into a large one and the yolks into a small one. Separate each egg very carefully; there should not be even the slightest bit of yolk in the whites. Add the salt to the egg whites and beat them until they are stiff; they will be ready when it is possible to cut into them with a knife or the blades of the beater and the impression is still there a few seconds later. Mix the plain sugar with the vanilla sugar and let it trickle into the egg whites, beating all the time. Sprinkle the lemon rind over the top and fold in gently.

Beat the egg yolks until they are pale and creamy. Add 2 tablespoons of the meringue to the egg yolks and mix together well. Let the yolks glide onto the surface of the remaining meringue. Do not fold in. Sift the flour over the top, and fold the mixture together very gently but thoroughly with a spatula. do not stir or the mixture will lose some of its lightness.

Heat the butter in an oval gratin dish until it starts to bubble. It should not becomes brown. Using two large spoons, lift one-third of the mixture at a time into the dish so that the three mounds (or

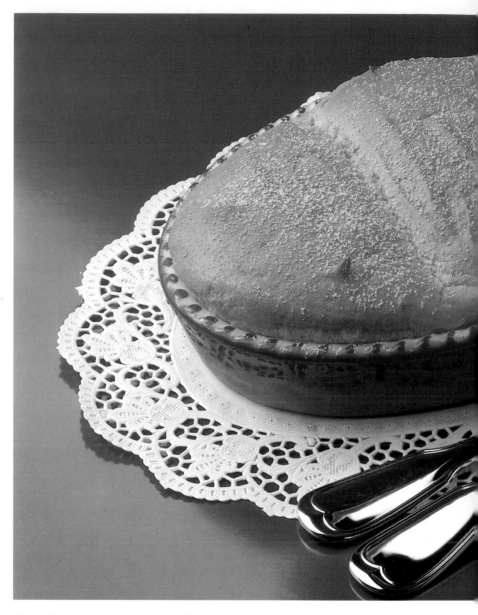

dumplings) are next to one another. Place in the heated oven immediately and bake for about 5 minutes, then reduce the temperature to 225°F and bake for a further 10 minutes or until the tops are light brown; the dumplings should still be creamy and soft inside.

Remove from the oven and dredge with sifted confectioners' sugar. Serve immediately since the dumplings will collapse at the slightest draft or if they have to wait. It is better to ask your guests to wait for the dumplings rather than the other way around!

1 **Adding the egg yolks to the meringue.** Beat the egg yolks in a second bowl and add 2 tablespoons of the meringue mixture. Mix well before letting the yolks glide onto the remaining meringue.

2 **Adding the flour.** Sift the flour over the top of the meringue and egg yolk mixtures. Fold together gently but thoroughly using a spatula. Do not stir or the mixture will lose some of its lightness.

3 **Placing the dumpling mixture in the dish.** Heat the butter in the dish. Remove one-third of the mixture at a time with two large spoons and place in three mounds in the dish.

Pashka

The decoration for this special Russian Easter dessert should be as rich as the ingredients.

Serves 8

---

1 cup unblanched almonds
10 tablespoons butter
1¾ cottage cheese
3 egg yolks
½ cup sugar
6 tablespoons heavy cream
⅓ cup raisins
3 tablespoons glacé cherries
¼ cup finely chopped candied lemon peel
¼ cup finely chopped candied orange peel
1–2 vanilla beans
⅔ cup mixed candied fruit for decoration

Preparation time: 1½ hours
To chill: 12–24 hours

Pashka is as much a part of the Russian Easter as painted eggs and vodka. Each family naturally has its own recipe but the pashka is always richly decorated and made in a special pyramid-shaped wooden form, perforated all around and lined with cheesecloth or muslin through which the excess liquid can drain. As such molds are difficult to find here, we suggest the use of a new clay flowerpot with a diameter of about 6 inches; this can be lined with a rectangular piece of cheesecloth or muslin measuring 36 × 40 inches.

Place the almonds in a bowl and pour boiling water over them. Leave to blanch for 3–5 minutes, then drain and rub off the skins between your fingers. Spread the nuts out on a clean dish towel and leave them to dry.

Cream the butter in a mixing bowl until softened. Gradually add the cottage cheese, beating it well so that the mixture becomes light and frothy. Set aside.

Beat the egg yolks with the sugar in the top of a double boiler over hot but not boiling water. Gradually beat in the cream. Continue to beat until the mixture becomes thick and creamy. Do not let it become too hot or the egg yolks will curdle. Remove the top pan from the pan of hot water and stand it in a bowl of cold water. Leave it to cool, beating vigorously from time to time.

Meanwhile, rinse the raisins in hot water and rub dry in a dish towel. Chop the glacé cherries coarsely or cut into quarters. Set aside one-third of the blanched almonds for the decoration, and finely chop the remainder. Mix the chopped almonds with the raisins, cherries, lemon peel and orange peel. Cut the vanilla beans open lengthwise and scrape out the pulp and seeds with a knife.

Pour the egg yolk and cream mixture into the butter and cheese mixture, followed by the mixed nuts and fruits and the vanilla pulp and seeds. Mix everything together lightly but thoroughly.

Rinse the flowerpot well in hot water. Fold the piece of cheesecloth or muslin together two or three times and dampen it. Use it to line the flowerpot, leaving a border of about 2 inches hanging over the rim all the way around. Stand a wire rack (or a cork cut into three equally thick slices) on a large soup plate and place the lined flowerpot on top, making sure the hole in the bottom of the pot is not blocked up. Balance the mixing bowl on the rim of the lined flowerpot so that it holds the cheesecloth in place and pour in the mixture. Fold the edges of the damp cheesecloth over the mixture all around and press down firmly.

First put a plate that exactly fits the flowerpot on top of the mixture, then stand a pot on this and fill it with water. Allow the pashka to firm up and dry out slightly in the refrigerator.

Before serving unfold the cheesecloth, place a large plate on top of the pashka and unmold it, as you would a cake. Remove the flowerpot and peel off the cheesecloth. Decorate the pashka generously with the candied fruits and reserved whole blanched almonds.

1 **Pouring in the mixture.** Balance the mixing bowl on the rim of the lined flowerpot so that it holds the cheesecloth lining in place, then pour in the mixture.

2 **Sealing the pashka.** Fold the overhanging cheesecloth up over the mixture all around the flowerpot and press it down firmly. Press carefully so the flowerpot does not tip over.

3 **Weighting the pashka.** Select a plate that will just fit inside the top of the flowerpot and place it on the mixture. Weight with a pot filled with water.

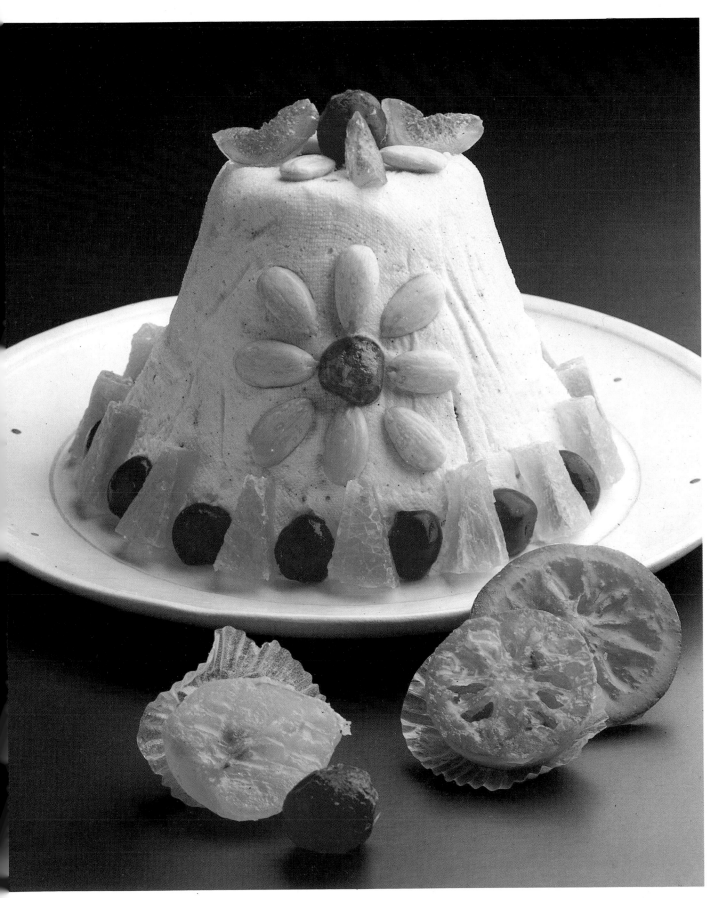

Glossary of Cooking Terms

Al dente of pasta, firm to the bite

Allumettes vegetables cut into matchstick-sized pieces

Antipasti cold or hot Italian hors d'oeuvre

A point referring to meat, medium cooked

Aspic a clear jelly made from the cooked, clarified juices of meat, chicken or fish

Bain marie or water bath, a large pan filled with hot water in which delicate dishes can be cooked, or kept warm

Bake blind to bake pastry cases without a filling. To help keep their shape they are first lined with parchment paper or foil and filled with dried beans or peas or bread crusts

Bard to cover lean meat, game or poultry with strips of fat to prevent the flesh drying out during cooking

Blanch to boil briefly in order to: set the color of food prior to freezing, or cooking by another method; loosen the skins of fruits or nuts to make peeling easier; remove unpleasant flavors and impurities

Bouquet garni a bunch or muslin bag of herbs and seasonings, often composed of sprigs of parsley, thyme, marjoram and bay, with a clove of garlic and black peppercorns

Braise to brown in hot fat, then simmer in a covered pan with vegetables and a seasoned liquid

Brine a salted water solution used for pickling and preserving

Brioche a rich yeast pastry or bread, slightly sweetened

Brûlé a term used to describe sweet dishes, such as custards, finished with a caramelized sugar glaze

Cannelloni pasta tubes, stuffed with a savory filling

Charlotte a hot pudding, consisting of a bread-lined mold filled with fruit; or a cold dessert, again using a mold (called a charlotte mold), this time lined with lady-fingers and filled with fruit and/or cream

Chantilly lightly sweetened whipped cream

Chaud-froid a formal, classic presentation made from meat, poultry, game or fish covered with a creamy sauce; often, too, coated with aspic and highly decorated

Chiffonade a garnish of shredded lettuce, sorrel or spinach, used to decorate soups or cold dishes

Clarify to "clear" butter or fats by heating, allowing to cool and settle then filtering; or to clear stock with beaten egg white, to make consommé

Cocotte small, ovenproof, porcelain or earthenware cooking dish, in which individual portions can be both cooked and served

Compote dessert of fresh or dried fruit, poached in syrup

Consommé a clear meat or fish stock, made as for ordinary stock, then clarified with beaten egg white

Court bouillon highly seasoned liquid in which fish are poached

Crêpe a thin pancake, sweet or savory

Custard a creamy sauce or base for a dessert made by cooking together egg yolks and milk or cream

Dariole small, smooth-sided mold used for making sweet and savory creams

Daube a stew of braised meat and vegetables

Deglaze to add stock or wine to pan juices and briefly cook together to make a sauce

Demi-glace a concentrated, rich brown gravy or sauce base

Dice to cut into small cubes

Dredge to dust or sprinkle food with flour or sugar

Dressing a sauce for a salad; or stuffing for poultry or boned meat

Dumpling a small, savory ball, often made from a stuffing or potato mixture; or a fruit-filled dough-based pudding

En papillote food wrapped and cooked in buttered parchment paper or foil parcel

Entrée a warm or cold dish served as part of a formal meal, where it follows the fish course and precedes the main course

Farce a filling for pies, terrines, meats, poultry, fish or vegetables, usually consisting of finely chopped or puréed meat, fish or vegetables, seasoned

Ficeler to tie up with string

Fines herbes	finely chopped herbs, used in various combinations, but often consisting of parsley, chervil, tarragon and chives
Flambé	food tossed, i.e. "flamed", in a pan to which burning brandy or other spirit has been added
Fleurons	small, half-moon-shaped puff pastries used to garnish savory dishes and soups
Fold in	to incorporate one ingredient into another, using a metal spoon or a spatula
Fond blanc	white veal or chicken stock
Fond de gibier	game stock
Fond de volaille	white poultry stock
Fricassee	a white stew, generally of veal, lamb or chicken cooked in stock and finished with cream and egg yolks
Fumet	a concentrated stock generally made from fish, but also from meat or vegetables
Galantine	a cold dish of boned and stuffed poultry, game or meat, generally glazed with aspic
Garnish	an edible decoration for a savory dish
Gelatin	a pure, tasteless bone extract in powder form which dissolves in hot liquid and forms a jelly when cold
Glace de viande	a highly reduced meat stock of veal, chicken, game or fish, used to improve sauces or glaze meats
Glaze	a glossy finish given to food by brushing with beaten egg (before cooking) or sweet syrup (after cooking)
Gratiner	to brown under the broiler to produce a crust
Gravy	a sauce made by boiling roasted meat or poultry juices with stock and/or wine, sometimes thickened with a little flour
Hors d'oeuvre	a hot or cold appetizer
Infuse	to steep ingredients in liquid to extract their flavor
Jug	to stew meat, for example jugged hare, in a covered pot
Julienne	fine strips of vegetable or truffle, included in or accompanying a dish
Jus	pure meat juice or roasting juices, used as a gravy
Lard	pork fat. *To lard*, to insert strips of pork fat into lean meat to keep it moist during cooking
Lardon	a small strip of pork fat
Lier	to thicken
Macerate	to soak a food in flavored liquid, to soften it
Marinade	a blend of oil, spices, herbs and other flavorings used to tenderize and flavor meat, game or fish
Mie de pain	white bread crumbs without crust
Mijoter	to simmer or braise over very low heat
Mirepoix	finely diced root vegetables, onion and bacon lightly fried in butter and used as a base for brown sauces and stews
Monter	to beat butter into a sauce or soup
Mousse	light sweet or savory cold dish made with cream, whipped egg white and gelatin
Nap	to mask, or cover, foods with aspic or sauce
Navarin	a stew of lamb and vegetables
Panada	a binding or thickening agent made of flour or bread
Paner	to dip first in flour, then in bread crumbs
Pâté	savory mixture, baked, either in a terrine or a pastry case, then served cold
Pâte feuilletée	puff pastry
Pickle	to preserve vegetables or fruit in brine or a vinegar solution
Poach	to cook slowly without allowing to boil
Primeurs	early or spring vegetables, early fruit, or young wine
Purée	raw or cooked food processed until smooth
Quenelle	a light, small savory dumpling made of meat or fish, served as a garnish or in a delicate sauce
Ragoût	a stew of chopped meat and vegetables
Reduce	to boil liquid such as stock, soup or sauce to thicken or concentrate it and enhance the flavor
Refresh	to cool boiled vegetables or meat under cold running water
Rémoulade	highly seasoned mayonnaise with chopped herbs, anchovy fillets, capers and gherkins
Rissolé	fried or baked until brown and crisp
Roast	to cook in the oven, on a spit or over an open fire
Roux	a blend of melted butter and flour, lightly cooked together and used as a base for savory sauces
Salmi	a stew made from roasted game
Sauter	to fry food quickly in little oil
Savarin	rich yeast cake, baked in a ring mold and then soaked in liqueur-flavored syrup
Skim	to remove scum from the surface of stock or broth
Soufflé	sweet or savory baked dish based on a sauce or purée, enriched with egg yolks, into which the beaten whites are then folded
Steam	to cook in steam without the food coming into contact with the liquid
Stew	to simmer food gently in a covered pan
Strain	to separate liquids from solids by passing them through a sieve or through cheesecloth
Stuff	to fill with a seasoned mixture (stuffing)
Terrine	an earthenware pot for cooking and serving pâté

Truss to tie a roast of meat or a bird into a compact shape with skewers, string, or both, before cooking

Vanilla sugar sugar flavored with vanilla beans

Velouté basic white sauce made from a *roux* base and veal, chicken or fish stock

Vinaigrette an emulsion of oil, vinegar and seasonings generally used as a salad dressing

Vol-au-vent light, puff pastry case (patty shell)

Zest oil in the outer skin or rind of citrus fruits, often grated or peeled to flavor sweet sauces and desserts

Index